The IB Economics Commentary:
Examples and Advice

The IB Economics Commentary:

Examples and Advice

ALEXANDER ZOUEV

ZOUEV PUBLISHING

This book is printed on acid-free paper.

Copyright © 2012 Alexander Zouev. All rights reserved.

No part of this book may be used or reproduced in any manner whatsoever without written permission, except in the case of brief quotations embodied in critical articles or reviews.

Published 2012

Printed by Lightning Source

ISBN 978-0-9560873-4-8, paperback.

"Economics is a subject that does not greatly respect one's wishes"

Nikita Khrushchev

TABLE OF CONTENTS

Introduction	1
The Article	3
Structure and Format	6
Diagrams	9
Assessment	12
Teacher Feedback	22
The Cover Page	24
Examples of Excellent Commentaries	26

INTRODUCTION

The IB Economics commentary is arguably one of the most interesting, yet most difficult internal assessments you will complete throughout your IB program. The aim of this short textbook is to show you what it takes to write a grade 7 commentary, as well as point out any potential pitfalls and give tips that will maximize your marks. This introductory chapter will review all of the basic information you need to know before starting your commentaries. Thereafter, we will look at where to find good articles, how to use the marking criteria to maximize marks, and also I will present a section on how best to deal with graphs and diagrams.

The IA is a vital part of the course and is compulsory for both SL and HL students. It allows students to demonstrate the application of their skills and knowledge and to pursue their personal interests, without the time limitations and other constraints associated with written examinations. The internal assessment requirements changed significantly for examinations starting 2013 and this book takes all of these changes into account.

The most significant change is that the portfolio of commentaries has been reduced from four to three – however each commentary still must be based on a different section of the course. Another change is the word count. As in the past, a commentary must not exceed 750 words, but the minimum number of words is now no longer specified.

What is the Economics Internal Assessment?

The IA in IB Economics is a written commentary which is based on an economics article or any published extract from news media that you yourself choose. In total, the IA for economics is a **portfolio of three commentaries**, each one no more than **750 words**. Each commentary must explain linkages between the extract and an economic theory taken from the section of the syllabus on which the commentary is based, as well as demonstrate economic insights into the implications of the extract. It should provide evidence of the student's ability to evaluate current events from the point of view of an economist.

Each commentary must focus on a different section of the IB Economics syllabus, although it is possible for commentaries to make a reference to other sections – such as a microeconomics focused commentary that alludes to macroeconomic policy. Teachers in some schools may make students write four commentaries, and then make the student choose the best three. The different sections are outlined below:

1. <u>Microeconomics</u> - E.g. Demand & Supply, Taxation, Market Failure, Theory of the Firm etc.
2. <u>Macroeconomics</u> - E.g. Unemployment, Inflation, Income Distribution, Economic growth etc.
3. <u>International Economics</u> - E.g. Comparative Advantage, Exchange Rate, Balance of Payments etc.
4. <u>Development Economics</u> - E.g. Human Development Index, Barriers to Development etc.

This IA is extremely important because of how much weight it will have on your final economics grade. For **Economics Standard Level** students, your IA now **represents 20%** of your total Economics score. For **Economics Higher Level** students, your IA also **represents 20%** of your total Economics score. This may not seem like much at the time, but if you think about it, these percentages are extremely important. 20% of a total possible 7 points is nearly 2 entire points! That's right; you can add 2 points to your entire IB total if you maximize your marks on these commentaries. Compare that to the 3 additional points you get out of a combination of the Extended Essay and Theory of Knowledge components and you will really see how invaluable these points are.

The fact of the matter is that the final economics exam can be tricky – very tricky. Even the most prepared students can stumble on the paper 1 questions, or run out of time for the paper 3. You must do everything you can to maximize your marks on the IA. Imagine you write three outstanding commentaries that you predict will score 18/20 or 19/20. This means you will basically be walking into the exam room with already 2 points secured towards your final grade. The feeling of confidence and assurance will go a long way to push you through the final exams.

As the weighing of the IA is rather high, this should be reflected in the amount of time you spend on creating the portfolio. The IBO recommends that 'a total of approximately 20 hours should be allocated to the portfolio at both SL and HL'. This includes time for the teacher to explain the requirements, class time for students, time for consultation and time to review and monitor the progress. The first piece of advice I'm going to share with you is probably one that you already know and don't want to hear repeated: get a head start! Commentaries should not be rushed the day before a deadline. You need to take your time and make it perfect.

The Article

The extracts on which each commentary is based must be drawn from four different sources. Extracts must be relatively modern and contemporaneous (not older than 6 months from time of writing). It's a good idea to note down any potential articles as you proceed throughout the school year. I'm sure that many of you check the daily news or read articles in magazines and newspapers to keep up with current events. Make sure to bookmark any article that you think you could potentially use in a future commentary.

For your first IA, you will need to pick an article on something that you have studied in class – this is most likely going to be something about supply/demand, elasticity, or market failure. More than half of the commentaries that I have come across as an economics tutor have dealt with the price of some commodity, usually coffee, oil, cocoa or something similar. I would recommend however that you choose something that revolves around a main topic, and is not too narrow.

I strongly recommend picking something simple. If you don't know what an article is saying, don't pretend to understand your way out of it. You will lose marks, and there are plenty of simple articles around. Moreover, the less complex articles will be better suited for the purpose of economic evaluation – something we will look into later.

Finding a good article is very important. Even if it takes you hours to find a good one, it's better to do that than quickly find a not-so-good one and realize that it's not suited for analysis. The general advice here is to find an article that doesn't say too much, and you can then fill in the blanks and expand. Finding an article will not be easy, because you have to consider a lot of sources before you find one that is suitable for you. It can be a headache, but with some patience you will be able to find one that suits you perfectly.

Where to look?

Back in the day when I was completing my Economics portfolio, there was this rumor going around that a paper source (newspaper, magazine) was somehow 'better' than something found online. Now with the newspaper industries struggling and the rise of iPads and other tablet readers that feature newspaper publications, this is no longer a concern. You can safely find articles online – as long as they are still from a reputable source.

The articles may be from a newspaper, a journal or the internet, but must not be from television or radio broadcasts. It is also discouraged for students to include articles that are too long, in which case they need to highlight the relevant bits.

The following sources might have appropriate articles:
- New York Times International Edition
- BBC News Online
- Reuters
- The Guardian
- thestar.com
- CNN Online
- Times of India
- Irish Times
- USnews.com

The Economist and the Financial Times are sources that you might expect to have good articles for economic analysis, but I believe the contrary is true. They usually do the economic analysis for you, and there is much less scope for evaluation because all of their articles are very well written and make points that are more difficult to argue against. In general, it is not advisable to take articles from any sort of business or economic newspaper because they will provide their own commentary already. The purpose of the IA is to find a news article and attempt to extract the economic theory and principles from that story.

Guidance

You should be able to judge for yourself if your article is appropriate. I'm hopeful that most Economics teachers will be able to give you the green light if you ask for their approval. Understandably, this will vary school to school as teachers are not explicitly obliged to provide approval. However I'm sure if you ask kindly enough and go see them after class hours they should be able to help.

Analyzing the Article

You need to get in a habit of reading economic articles much like you would do in your Paper 3 exams. This means reading them very carefully, and noting key words and statements. I suggest you highlight everything that you might potentially quote – and you should even submit your article like this as it shows that you have made the effort to analyze before starting your commentary. Also note that if you have a very long article, highlight the relevant parts of it so the examiner knows what is important.

Once you have picked an article, you will need to analyze it. If your article is about a change in the price of a commodity (as most first commentaries will be), you should ask yourself questions such as: why did the price change? Can I use a supply and demand diagram to explain this? By how much did quantity change? Who was affected by the price change? Keep in mind that 750 words is not much. The key to writing a great commentary is finding that perfect balance between introduction, body, evaluation, diagrams and analysis, and concluding remarks. Make every word count, and don't waste sentences on things that are just not worth it.

STRUCTURE AND FORMAT

For many students, starting an economics commentary is very difficult. Here is a simple approach to get you going. First, you need to summarize the article in a line or two. Thereafter, define some of the key terms which will be relevant to your discussion (again, just use your textbook/notes for the definitions and copy them out word for word). Then, in one sentence, try to summarize what your analysis is going to ultimately say (what effect the event has had/ will have). The introduction needs to be short and to the point, 5 lines at most. Opening sentences effectively talk about the summary of the news article – they give a very clear and precise outline of what will be discussed to the examiner. Then you could have a progressive sentence that outlines the link to economic theory. The last bit of your introduction could be a closing sentence that tells the examiner which economic theory you will comment on.

Avoid the 'scatter gun' approach, where you write about everything you think might be related, and hope to eventually hit the nail on the head. You should choose a few issues which are at the heart of the article and go for a precise and concentrated approach. The body paragraphs of your commentary have no general formula which you need to abide by, so feel free to be flexible. It may be more beneficial to have a coherent layout and talk about each theory separately.

The main body of your commentary will be dealing with the analysis and the diagrams. You **must** have a diagram. Diagrams are quintessential to IB Economics, so draw diagrams – the more the merrier as long as they are justified. See the following chapter on diagrams for more advice and tips.

Before you dive into structuring you commentary, it may be a good idea to plan a rough outline. A good outline should identify the topic that you plan to write about (which section of the syllabus it will apply to). You should then proceed to identify the terms that you will likely define in your commentary, and get the definitions ready. Thereafter, think about which diagrams you will most likely use in your commentary. It is a very good idea to revise the theory fully before you start writing. Finally, you should have in mind already a few points you will make during your evaluation (see notes on evaluation later).

In your first paragraph, you should be looking to define several economic terms that you will talk about later. The subsequent paragraphs could be separated by each theory or section you will be analyzing. You should get used to referencing the article when developing a point or analyzing. Referencing does not need to be done like you would do in your Extended Essay – just write the referenced quote in the paragraph and don't worry about anything else. You should also avoid using any overly complicated vocabulary. Try to keep the commentary simple and easy to read.

When you get to your conclusion, you should keep this bit about the same length as the introduction. Four to five lines will be sufficient, as you should earn the most marks from your analysis in the body of the commentary. You could start with a summary sentence, where you mention the theories that you have analyzed and evaluated – no need to be detailed. The concluding sentence of your commentary could be something of personal opinion, or a recommendation of policy.

It goes without saying that the font, general format and style should be constant throughout the commentaries. Remember your portfolio will be graded as a whole, so it needs to be consistent. I recommend to keeping the standard margins that are set for a Word document, and not try to squeeze everything on one page. Whether you choose to indent the paragraphs or to use double spacing is up to you, but generally I find the more your commentary looks like a serious piece of academic work, the better. I don't think you can go wrong with Cambria font, size 11, no indentation, and single spacing between paragraphs (and full justify). It looks very neat, and is my preferred weapon on choice when writing almost any type of paper for university or school.

With regards to typography and font emphasis, I suggest the following. Use **bold** when you come across an economic term you will define, and then use parentheses for the definition. Use quotations and *italics* when quoting directly from the article. Lastly, whenever you refer to a diagram in your text, use the underline tool (e.g. <u>diagram 1</u>) and then underline the diagram titles as well. All of these techniques are simply shortcuts to signal to the examiner that you are making a deliberate attempt to score highly on the grading criteria, as we will see later.

I have seen some teachers suggest to their students to take this one step further and implement colors as another tool to secure marks. For example, some students opt to choose the font color blue when discussing economic principles, and then green when evaluating the article – thereby directly addressing two more areas on the grading criterion. Whether you wish to do this is up to you. I would only strongly recommend it if your teacher has brought it up, or is aware of what you are trying to do.

There are some teachers who recommend listing the word count at the end of your commentary, within the commentary itself. I don't think that this is essential, as it is not asked for in the official IB criterion (the word count only needs to be listed on the cover page). The choice here is yours, really. With regards to outside references, I would strongly try to avoid referencing anything that is not your own article. You only have 750 words to work with, so it would be hard to justify using more outside information. Any definitions you use that come from the IB syllabus or your textbook, you should not source. Try to avoid using the internet to find more information on the article, or referencing economic information not from your textbook. These things are certainly not recommended.

You should include quotes correctly. Remember that this is in a way a type of Paper 3 question where you are analyzing a text. You must refer back to the article if you want the examiner to know that you are actually analyzing what is written and not just writing out standard economic theory

DIAGRAMS

Diagrams are everything when it comes to IB Economics. Whether you are completing a simple homework assignment, answering a past exam question, or busy working on your IA, you can be sure of one thing – diagrams will be needed. In this section, I wish to explain how to best use diagrams in your commentaries, and give advice on how to construct them.

As you will see in the next section, diagrams are of upmost importance in your IA. So much so, that they have their own grading criterion, where you can score up to a maximum of 3 marks. That means diagrams are worth nearly 20% of your entire commentary mark. Moreover, this means that you **absolutely must** have **at least one** diagram in your commentary. My recommendation is it's safer to have at least two, but don't overdo it and certainly no more than 6 or 7. If you have the choice between explaining something in one diagram or splitting it into two, I would go with the latter option.

My first piece of advice as to how to create your diagrams is to **go big**. Don't bother making something small and clustering it with arrows and text. Use the entire width of the page, and make them clear and visible. Some students have a strong temptation to draw the diagrams by hand; however I don't recommend this for a few reasons. First of all, as I will explain in the next paragraph, creating a diagram in Microsoft word or any word processing program is not difficult at all. It will look neat and professional, and you can easily copy and paste the diagram if you plan on re-using it to show any shifts or changes. To say that drawing a diagram by hand will be 'good practice' is not really a legitimate reason. You will get enough practice drawing diagrams by hand when doing past papers. In the IA, the key is to make diagrams neat and accurate – as if they are coming straight from the textbook.

The best diagrams are ones that borrow **actual facts and figures** from the text. For example, if prices went up from $1.53/kg to $1.88/kg then use these as points on your price axis. If the tax was an 11% increase, then label the arrow next to your tax shift '11% tax rise'. Teachers and examiners love this. It really shows that you have read your article and are confident enough to build diagrams that incorporate data directly from the text. It also shows a level of effort that surpasses diagrams that are simply copied and pasted from textbooks/online. Now, understandably, this will not always be possible as some articles will not have prices and figures that you can incorporate. Nonetheless, if you think you have an opportunity to do so, don't pass up on it.

Building Diagrams in Microsoft Word

Personally, I found MS Word to be absolutely fine in terms of drawing the diagrams. You don't have to be a particularly tech-savvy person to get to grips with the drawing tools; however I would like to share a few bits of advice to make your life easier. Let's pretend I have to draw a diagram illustrating the effects of pollution. The first thing I would do is create a **canvas** [Insert -> Shapes -> New Drawing Canvas]. This is basically going to be your working space. The benefits of having a Canvas are two-fold. First of all it means all of your lines and textboxes will be contained within that canvas and not interfere with the text in the body of the commentary. Any formatting or changes you make will not affect what is contained within the canvas. The second benefit is that if you happen to need a similar diagram to the one you just used, albeit with a small shift or change, then you can simply copy and paste the canvas and that will duplicate all of the shapes and text inside.

Once you have your canvass, adjust the size of it to whatever you like. I strongly recommend filling up at least half the page, and certainly the whole width. Now add a textbox diagram inside, and using a small font, name the diagram whatever you want it to be (for example, Figure 1: *Effects of Pollution*). Make sure the textbox is transparent (no fill) and has no outline [Format -> Shape Fill/Shape Outline]. This ensures that your textboxes don't cover up any of the diagram and don't have any ugly borders. For your axis labels I suggest using an even smaller font size. Make sure that titles do not exceed 10 words and labels do not exceed 5 words – otherwise it will be included in your word count.

To draw the axis of the diagram is very simple. Go Insert->Shapes and choose the straight line (whether you want/need the arrowed line is up to you). Now when you are making your axis, hold down **Shift** as you draw – this ensures that you are drawing a straight 0, 45 degree, or 90 degree line. Your main axis will mostly be two lines – a horizontal and a vertical one. As far as the main lines in your diagram (supply, demand, etc.) are concerned, you will also use the straight line drawing tool. Now however, you should experiment with color and thickness [Format -> Shape Outline -> Weight/Dashes]. I recommend making any lines that connect to the axis and indicate points along the main line in thin dashes.

One of the most common complaints I hear from students who use MS Word to draw diagrams is to do with the rigid movements of the objects. This problem is easily solved. You must ensure that 'object snapping' is turned off – then you will be able to move lines pixel by pixel as opposed to awkward spaces. To do this, go to Format -> Align -> Grid Settings and uncheck 'Snap Objects to Grid Lines'. Now just use your keyboards arrow keys to shift things by the slightest amount. Simple!

Make an effort to really explore the drawing tools that MS Word has on offer. Whatever your needs, there will be some solution. For example, curved lines (such as LRAS) can be drawn using the curved line tool and then rotated, expanded, and shifted. You can use triangles and boxes to replicate the shading effect found in certain diagrams (such as welfare loss) – just format the shapes shading. In the end you will be able to build diagrams such as the one below in less than 10 minutes.

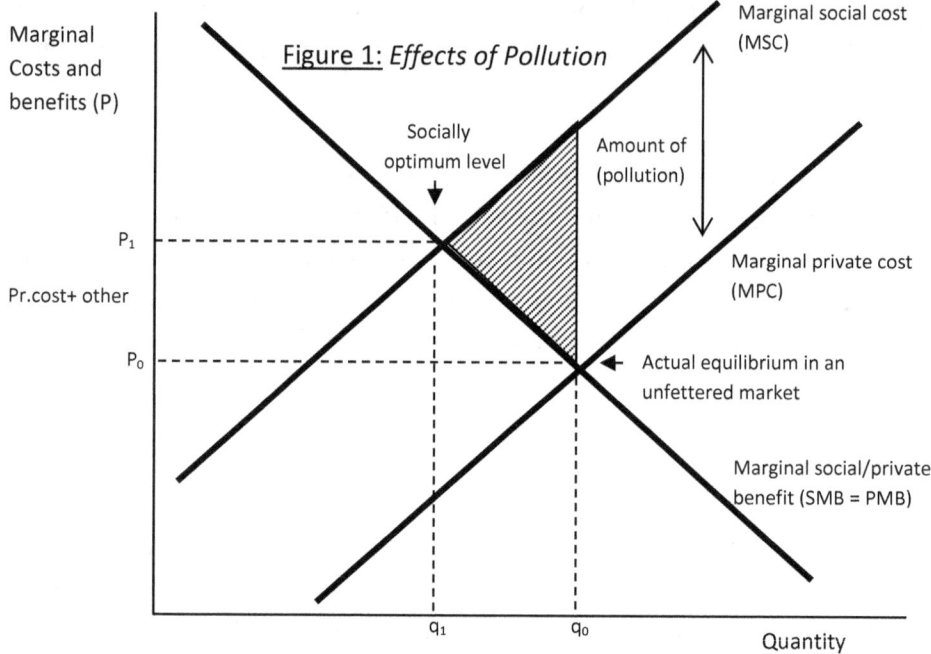

Explore the other functions and options in MS Word – such as grouping, which will allow your shapes to stay in place even within the canvas. The key is not let your diagrams be limited by anything. Word can make your diagrams look as professional and as pretty as you imagine – you just need to find out the solution. So far in this section I have covered the major slip-ups, but if you discover something that still bothers you, try to Google it and I'm positive that you will find a solution.

Assessment

If you are the lazy type and chose to skip the first few sections of this book, then please read this section with 100% focus. This is what it all boils down to – everything else is almost irrelevant in comparison. At the end of the day, the only thing that will matter is how well you do on the IB assessment scale. I have reproduced the official assessment criteria that will be used by your teachers and examiners and we will now go through each section step-by-step to figure out how to score maximum marks along the way.

The first thing to note about the grading of this IA is that the entire portfolio is graded against the rubric in a holistic manner – individual commentaries are not graded one by one, but as a whole portfolio. This means that you need to be consistent across all of your commentaries. Use the same formatting, same design of diagrams, same layout and similar tone. Also this should incentivize you to pay close attention to detail across all commentaries. Just because your first two were excellent, doesn't mean you should slack on the remainder.

For internal assessment, a number of assessment criteria have been identified. Each assessment criterion has level descriptors describing specific levels of achievement together with an appropriate range of marks. Your teacher must judge the work against the criteria using the level descriptors.

There are five internal assessment criteria for each commentary and one internal assessment criterion for the portfolio as a whole. Each commentary is assessed individually for the first five assessment criteria (A – E) and then criterion F is applied to the whole portfolio. The maximum for the portfolio is 45 marks (14 marks x 3 commentaries = 42, plus 3 marks). Now let's take a look at these criterions in more detail.

Criterion A: Diagrams

This criterion assesses the extent to which the student is able to construct and use diagrams.

Level	Descriptor
0	The work does not reach a standard described by the descriptors below
1	Relevant diagrams are included but not explained, or the explanations are incorrect.
2	Relevant, accurate and correctly labeled diagrams are included, with a limited explanation
3	**Relevant, accurate** and **correctly labeled diagrams** are included, with a **full explanation**.

In the world of IB Economics, diagrams are everything. A lot of the information in here I will have covered in the section on Diagrams, which should be read first. We are paying specific attention to the grade descriptors. Note the key words used in the top descriptor: *relevant, accurate, and correctly labeled*. Let's start with relevant. This simply means that you are using the correct diagram to show what you are describing in the text. You use a supply and demand diagram when talking about a price rise in a product, and not, as some students have in the past, some macroeconomic diagram with an aggregate supply and aggregate demand curve. If you have any doubt about the 'relevance' of your diagrams, then it's best to leave them out and reconsider the main points of your commentary.

The word *'accurate'* is also very straight-forward. You may be using the relevant diagrams, but unless you are shifting your curves the right way, or have curves sloping in the right direction, you could lose marks. An easy way to avoid this pitfall and to score highly in this category in general, is just to replicate the diagrams from your IB Economics textbook. Obviously you need to create these yourselves (see the relevant section about creating diagrams) and adjust them to include any information you can gather from the text.

'Correctly labeled' should not be overlooked. Too often students mix up the supply curve with the demand curve, or consumer surplus with producer surplus. Once again, this issue can be avoided completely if you just stick to replicating the diagrams from the textbook and eliminate carelessness. The biggest issue here is simply an omission of labeling. Students have a tendency to just leave curves unmarked, or forget to specify where Q1 or Q2 are. My advice with regards to this is to rather be better safe than sorry. You should label everything you possibly can – a zero at the origin, curves that you have labeled before, anything else that might be important.

More importantly, 'correctly labeled' implies that your diagrams have proper labels! Saying something like Fig.1.1 is not enough. Try to be as precise as you can, e.g. 'Fig1.1 – The Effect of A shift in the Demand Curve for Brazilian Cocoa'. Each of your diagrams should have a name, a number, and title (Fig XX: Title) – this way even the harshest of examiners can't downgrade you in this respect. Personally I also prefer students to avoid shorthand notation and use the full names where appropriate. Obviously for things like quantities you would use Q1 and Q2, but when it comes to labeling the axis and the curves, I highly recommend you write out the full names (e.g. Supply Curve instead of S, Price Level instead of P).

The last bit of the descriptor demands that diagrams have 'a full explanation'. This is actually referring to the fact that students often simply throw a diagram in the middle of a paragraph and never allude to it in the text itself. Always make sure you have sentences like 'this affected x by because of the shift in the y curve and this can be seen **in the diagram below**'. Examiners hate to see students simply cut and paste a diagram and expect the reader to know what is going on and to which part of the text the diagram is related to. Of course the examiners will more often than not know exactly what you are doing, but you have to treat this commentary as a serious work of academic journalism, and as such, always explain things clearly and coherently.

Criterion B: Terminology

This criterion assesses the extent to which the student uses appropriate economic terminology

Level	Descriptor
0	The work does not reach a standard described by the descriptors below
1	Terminology relevant to the article is included in the commentary
2	**Terminology relevant** to the article is **used appropriately throughout** the commentary

Criterion B is rather straightforward. Here we are mainly dealing with definitions and explanation of economic concepts. My best advice is to first scan your article for any economic terms already in there (supply, tax, inflation, etc.) – these words you absolutely must define somewhere in your commentary. In fact, any economic terms you use, you better make sure you provide an accurate (just use the textbook glossary) definition. Personally I prefer students to put the **economic terms in bold** and then directly thereafter use parentheses for the definition. This makes it easy for the examiner to locate the terminology, and quickly check the definition you have used. Remember, you want to make the examiners life as easy as possible.

In this criterion, the middle descriptor demands that you simply *include* relevant terminology – something that everybody can do effortlessly. The key is to use the terminology *appropriately*. To be on the safe side, I would be looking to define at least 4 economic terms per commentary, and no more than 7 or 8 (you want to have enough words left for the other stuff). If you do that, and use the official definition as used by IB Economics, then you can safely secure the 2 maximum marks. If you use a term and think it might need to be defined, just define it.

Criterion C: Application

This criterion assesses the extent to which the student recognizes, understands and applies economic information in the context of the article.

Level	Descriptor
0	The work does not reach a standard described by the descriptors below
1	Relevant economic concepts and/or theories are applied to the article
2	**Relevant economic concepts** and/or theories are **applied appropriately throughout** the article

This criterion is a bit ambiguous. It's hard to understand what they mean by 'relevant concepts' and/or 'theories'. To most examiners, as long as you picked an article that allowed for economic analysis which comes directly from your syllabus, then those economic concepts are relevant.

There are no real shortcuts to getting all 2 points from the top descriptor. It really is a mix of how well you understand the economic information in the article, and are you convincing enough. As long as you avoid making false statements and provide reasonable arguments and justifications, I think it isn't too hard to get top marks.

Criterion D: Analysis

This criterion assesses the extent to which the student can explain and develop appropriate economic theories and/or concepts in the context of the article.

Level	Descriptor
0	The work does not reach a standard described by the descriptors below
1	There is limited economic analysis relating to the article
2	There is appropriate economic analysis relating to the article
3	There is **effective economic analysis relating** to the article

As with the previous criterion, criterion D is also a little wishy-washy. The wording in the top criterion simply demands 'effective economic analysis relating to the article'. To me this leaves a lot of room for personal preference and interpretation, both on the side of teacher and moderator. I think the best advice to score highly on this criterion (and it is important you do, as it is worth 3 marks) is to make it clear to the reader that you are purposely attempting economic analysis. Statements such as 'paragraph 2 clearly alludes to the benefits of direct taxes, which I will now demonstrate…'. If you do that once or twice, the examiner can rest assure that you are making a direct attempt at analysis. Sometimes it may be even safer to use the words directly from the descriptor: 'paragraph 2 clearly alludes to the benefits of direct taxes, my *economic analysis* of this concept is shown in the diagram below where…' This is a favorite trick of mine when it's hard to tell what the descriptor really demands. Using the IB's own terminology can surprisingly score you some easy marks.

Criterion E: Evaluation

This criterion assesses the extent to which the student synthesizes his or her analysis in order to make judgments that are supported by reasoned arguments.

Level	Descriptor
0	The work does not reach a standard described by the descriptors below
1	Judgments are made that are unsupported, or supported, by incorrect reasoning.
2	Judgments are made that are supported by limited reasoning
3	Judgments are made that are supported by appropriate reasoning
4	**Judgments** are made that are supported by **effective and balanced reasoning**

This is the big one. Evaluation will separate the great students, from the mediocre students, from the poor students. Not only is worth nearly 30% of your entire IA mark, but it is also the criterion on which it is the hardest to score full marks. In evaluation you must evaluate the theory and it's assumptions that you have chosen to apply with regards to the article.

Evaluation is important not just for your IA, but you will need to show evidence of evaluation throughout your exam papers as well. My general advice for evaluation is not too dissimilar from what the IBO recommends in their official IB Economics textbook, which I have reprinted below. There are **four** key ways in which you can show evaluative skills:

i) Compare Advantages and Disadvantages: this is probably the easiest way to evaluate – contrasting the 'good' and the 'bad' of a particular policy. This is a useful step in evaluation, but is not enough on its own. In order to complete the process, you need to make conclusions about the relative weight of the advantages or disadvantages.

Example 1: *'This shows that there are several advantages of protectionism in international trade. However, in terms of global resource allocation, the disadvantages outweigh the advantages and justify the efforts of the WTO to liberalize international trade"*

Example 2: *"As the diagram shows, the clear advantage of a minimum wage is that it can increase unemployment. However, the advantage of a minimum wage is that workers earn a reasonable wage, and this may outweigh the increase in unemployment"*

ii) Prioritize the Arguments: instead of just listing points, you could make a concluding statement in which you state which one is more (or less) significant or important and explain why.

Example 1: *"The most important argument against protectionism in international trade is that it represents a global misallocation of resources. This is because when countries erect protectionist barriers, they are supporting inefficient domestic producers at the expense of more efficient producers in foreign countries that are exploiting their comparative advantage"*

Example 2: *"The least effective way to effectively reduce the negative effects of smoking is to increase taxes. This is because the demand for cigarettes is inelastic and the increase in price due to taxes is likely to result in a proportionally smaller fall in quantity demanded. However, the government may earn high tax revenue which can be used to pay for the external costs and finance no-smoking campaigns."*

iii) Long Run vs. Short Run: it is quite common for the short-run consequences of an economic policy or event to be different from the long-run consequences. If you differentiate between the two time frames, you are showing evidence of evaluating.

Example 1: *"In the short run, abnormal profits can be earned in perfect competition. However, in the long run this is not possible. The existence of abnormal profits, perfect information, and lack of barriers to entry means that industry supply will increase, driving down the price taken by individual firms so that only normal profits may be earned."*

Example 2: *"In the short run, it may be possible to justify the infant industry argument as it is possible that, protected by tariffs, some firms will develop the economies of scale necessary to be internationally competitive. However, the danger is that in the long run, the industry will not become internationally competitive due to the lack of effective competition."*

iv) Consider the Stakeholders: a stakeholder is a person or group that has an investment, or interest in something'. In terms of IB Economics, stakeholders refer to domestic producers, consumers, foreign producers high-income people, low-income people, the government, or businesses.

Example 1: *"A high exchange rate may be good for consumers because it makes imported goods less expensive and forces domestic producers to be more efficient so that they compete with the less expensive imports. On the other hand it is clearly a disadvantage for those domestic producers who suffer from the competition from imports which become less expensive with the higher value of the currency"*

Example 2: *"Supply-side policies may be very good in terms of creating a more flexible labor force and achieving economic growth. However, they may lower the standard of living of workers who may suffer from deregulation of the labor laws.*

In addition, you can also **question the validity** of a certain statement made in the article. Usually, if your article is taken from a non-specialist paper, there may be statements made which contradict the basics that you learn in IB Economics. Be warned, however, that if the article is from somewhere like The Economist, it is safe to say that whatever they are claiming is probably more correct than what your basic economics suggests. This approach is risky, however it signals to the examiner that you have enough confidence in your understanding of economics to question the conclusions reached, and this makes for perfect evaluation.

You need to evaluate economic concepts or theories in the context of real world examples. The examiner will be asking whether you can judge an economic theory and an application to a given situation with awareness that the theory may not provide an accurate description. Phrases such as 'economic theory would suggest that x would happen, but as we see in this example, reality may be different'. Keep in mind the assumptions that are made within the IB Economics syllabus. For example, when a demand curve shifts in one direction, keep in mind that you are usually assuming all other factors are being kept constant. Or, for example, trade theory of comparative advantage is based on a variety of assumptions that don't actually hold up in real life.

Useful phrases which you should implement from time to time as evidence of attempted evaluation include:

- ✓ On the other hand…
- ✓ However, in the short/long run
- ✓ The most important concern is …. because …
- ✓ …. is somewhat insignificant compared to …
- ✓ In reality, the theory may not hold true because …
- ✓ This idea is often criticized for …

Do not rush your evaluations – they will make or break your portfolio. The article should be your invitation to analyze and evaluate how the situation is better understood through the lens of economic theory. Don't be afraid to question the economic theories presented in your textbooks either, and then use this as evaluation in your commentary. For example, one of the assumptions of production externalities is that the costs of the externality are easy to measure and quantifiable. In reality, the value of the spillover cost is only an estimate therefore suggesting a value of a tax that fully internalizes the externality is very difficult or near impossible. Another example (in macroeconomics) is that the four main central macro objectives which every government pursues are sometimes counterintuitive. For example, when pursuing increased growth, it is likely that the economy will experience increased inflationary pressure. If you make comments like this throughout your commentary then you will be showing to the examiner that you are capable of intelligent evaluative thought.

The debate of whether to spread evaluation throughout the article or leave it to the end comes up in classrooms every year. I don't think evaluations are left to the end on purpose, but I think by the time that you get the introduction, the theory and the diagrams out of the way; you are beyond the halfway point of your 750 word commentary. If you can evaluate throughout, by all means go ahead.

Criterion F: Rubric requirements

This criterion assesses the extent to which the student meets the five rubric requirements for the complete portfolio:

- ✓ Each commentary does not exceed 750 words
- ✓ Each article is based on a different section of the syllabus
- ✓ Each article is taken from a different and appropriate source
- ✓ Each article was published no earlier than one year before the writing of the commentary
- ✓ The summary portfolio coversheet, three commentary coversheets and the article for each commentary are included

Level	Descriptor
0	The work does not reach a standard described by the descriptors below
1	Three rubric requirements are met
2	Four rubric requirements are met
3	**All five** rubric requirements are met

This criterion is very straightforward. There is really no excuse for not securing all three points. Note that although this criterion is only applied once to the portfolio as a whole, it is important that you complete the requirements on each individual commentary as you go along. The article requirements are easy to fulfill, as long as you know what it needed. The coversheet requirements should be proof-read at the end, and usually the teacher will assist with the coversheets.

With regards to the world limit, students should be very careful not to go over the limit. Moderators are instructed not to read beyond 750 words, and more importantly, you will automatically be limited to score only 2 out of the possible 3 points in this criterion. Here is what the IB does **NOT** include in the IA Economics word count:

- Acknowledgements
- Contents page
- Diagrams

- Labels – of five words or fewer
- Headings on diagrams – of 10 words or fewer
- Tables of statistical data
- Equations, formulae and calculations
- Citations (which must be in the body of the commentary)
- References (which must be in the footnotes/endnotes)

Moreover, 'footnotes/endnotes may be used for references only'. Definitions of economic terms and quotations, if used, must be in the body of the work and are included in the word count. I would highly discourage trying to be too clever about the word count and fitting in chunks of writing into your diagrams, or squeezing text into citations so as to bypass the word count. 750 words is more than enough to write a grade 7 commentary, don't try to make up in quantity what you may lack in quality.

Once you have run through this assessment criteria once, make sure to check your commentary again. Be as critical as you can. It may only take you 10 or 20 minutes, but proofreading your work is very important when it comes to coursework.

Teacher Feedback

As IA's are part of the formal assessment (and moderated by the IBO), teachers are understandably not allowed to provide much assistance with the AI's. They are not allowed to reveal the marks they give (although some teachers will get around this and give you a grade on an A-F scale, thereby bypassing the IB grading system). The IB explicitly states that 'written feedback should generally be limited to reflecting on and explaining the instructions in the syllabus – define, label, explain etc.' So although teachers are allowed to point what makes sense and what doesn't, they are not supposed to give detailed instructions to students about how to improve their IA.

At the end of the day each commentary in the portfolio will be assessed individually against the internal assessment criteria by your Economics teacher. The teacher will initially assess each student's work. Thereafter, a **sample** of the work will be moderated by the IB. This usually means a few portfolios from the bottom-end, a few average ones, and a couple top portfolios will be send off and moderated. Personally, I don't like this approach because it still leaves too much in the hands of the individual teacher – who may or may not be qualified enough to assess these portfolios. I think that bias and student preference also play a part more often than one would expect.

This will be controversial, but I think there will be times when you need to make a trade-off between satisfying your teacher's demands and satisfying what a typical IB moderator will think of your commentary. Let's say you have teacher that is hell-bent on you doing things a certain way that isn't exactly mentioned anywhere in the criterion or official IB documentation. Let's say for example, the teacher demands that you have a clear and labeled section for introduction, analysis, evaluation and conclusion. Now, you know that this isn't a requirement, and moreover, you can write an excellent economics commentary without necessarily doing it this way. So what do you do? Abide by your school teachers set formula, or go about what the criterion and the advice in this book suggest?

Thinking about logically will probably lead you to side with your teacher. At the end of the day, it is rumored that when the IBO do moderate assessments, the grades do not swing by *that* much. This is of course relatively speaking. Let's observe the following two scenarios. In scenario one, you do everything the way your teacher likes, and you score 19/20. The IB then receives a sample of work from your school and decides that it's inflated, so they moderate it down two or maybe three marks: you are left with 16/20. Scenario two is that you go about what you think is excellent and follow the criterion and official IB documentation word for word. Your teacher doesn't recognize this, and penalizes you for not doing things his/her way – you get 10/20. Now when the work gets submitted, the moderation upwards is by a similar amount that it was downwards. So, in the best case scenario you end up with 13/20. I'd like to believe that moderators will give work the grade that the work truly deserves, but I am inclined to think that there is always a downward bias when it comes to moderators. Examiners are harsher when downgrading than they are lenient when upgrading.

In an ideal world examiners and local school teachers would be on the same page, and discrepancies between assessments would be minimal, if at all. Unfortunately, we do not live in an ideal world, and the problem of the clueless IB teacher will persist as long as new schools are adopting the program and hiring teachers without adequate training and experience. You need to make the best of the situation and make the right decision. At the end of the day, this is not something you should be worrying too much about. The most important thing is to focus on writing an excellent commentary, and then hoping for the best.

THE COVER PAGE

Unless your teacher provides you with a cover page to fill in, you can use the template I have created on the following page. The following information is **must** be included on each cover page:

- ✓ Title of extract
- ✓ Source of extract
- ✓ Date of extract
- ✓ Word count
- ✓ Date commentary was written
- ✓ Section of the syllabus to which the commentary relates

COMMENTARY COVER SHEET

Economics commentary number: _____

Title of extract: _____

Source of extract: _____

Date of extract: _____

Word count: _____ words

Date the commentary was written: _____

Section of the syllabus to which the commentary relates: _____

Candidate name: _____

Candidate number: _____

Examples of
Excellent Commentaries

*The commentaries featured in this section have all been part of portfolios that after being moderated by the IBO have achieved a grade 7.
**For copyright reasons, we were unable to include the original article extracts
*** We do not retain the copyright of these commentaries. They are being re-printed with the permission of the original authors.

1. 'Asking to be Taxed and Regulated'

This article focuses on the concept of negative externalities of pollution from a coal burning company called Cinergy and how they plan to deal with this problem. An **externality** occurs when there is a divergence between social and private costs and benefits. The **private cost** is the price of an activity to the individual producer – in this case the cost of running the power plants that Cinergy owns. In the diagram below we can see that free market allocation (considering only the private costs to Cinergy) would settle at q0.

The **social cost** however is the total cost of an activity to both the individual consumer/firm and rest of society as well. Social cost is equal to the private cost plus the externality. **Negative externalities** are spill-over effects that arise from the production or consumption of goods and services that have had no specific compensation. With negative externalities, like pollution, the social cost is greater than the private cost. The 56 million metric tons of carbon dioxide that the company Cinergy spews is the negative externality in this article and its costs are borne by society as a whole. The socially optimum allocation is at q1 where the social marginal cost = social marginal benefit. In the diagram we can see that firms such as Cinergy will not consider social costs and will overproduce. Cinergy produces too much compared to the socially optimal level. In the diagram we can see that on units q_0q_1 the social marginal cost is greater than the social marginal benefit, therefore there is allocative inefficiency (market failure). **Allocative efficiency** is where no resources are wasted – when no one can be made better off without making someone else worse off.

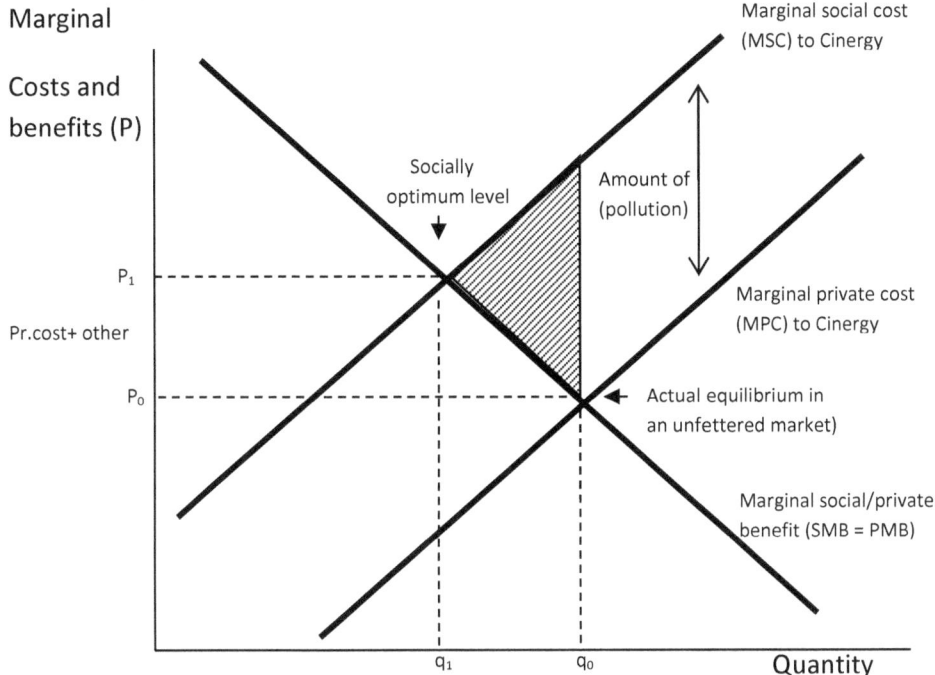

When the CEO of Cinergy, Jim Rogers, claims he 'is an outspoken advocate of regulating carbon and imposing a price on emissions' he is admitting that he realizes the pollution that his company is responsible for. His proposals of a 'regulatory scheme that would force power companies to cut carbon emissions' and spending '$1 billion to increase the use of cleaner-burning natural gas' can be seen as an attempt to get closer to the social optimum level of production. In the diagram, we can see that if Cinergy cuts its carbon emissions and cuts reliance on coal from 87% to 73% (from q_0 to q_1) it moves its marginal private level of production closer to the social optimum level of production (where MSC = MSB). The aim is to reduce the negative externality, and regulation is one way. The taxation mentioned in the articles title refers to the idea that if carbon is taxed, then the **indirect tax** (a fee charged by the government on a product/activity) lowers supply, which then raises the price to P_1 and lowers quantity supplied to q_1. This tax can be viewed as a pollution tax, it reduces the rate of new carbon dioxide that Cinergy releases (as represented by the fall to q_1)

The author is correct when mentioning that regulating and taxing Cinergys carbon emissions will help the environment, but overlooks the fact that the problem with these solutions is assessing the actual value of the negative externality, more specifically how much damage has already been done by the carbon emissions. Also the problem with taxing Cinergy, as the article mentions, is who has suffered from the CO2 may never be compensated. However that being said, the tax revenue could be used to clean up some of the pollution already produced. The article also mentions a merger (with Duke Energy), but fails to mention that if the companies merge they're going be a dominant player in the energy industry and will be able to influence the regulations set out by the government. The author has overlooked the idea that maybe the only reason Cinergy's CEO proposes all these ideas is because Cinergy already has a somewhat poor environmental reputation after 'backing away from a 1.4 billion settlement over alleged violations of the Clean Air Act'. For example if people are aware that Cinergy is concerned with the environment, they could favor it more over other power companies. The author fails to mention that by introducing what is known as tradable permits, Cinergy can purchase permits to pollute from firms who find it easier to reduce pollution. Overall the article introduces good ideas, but one must realize the difficulties in assessing the value of the negative externality.

2. "Oil Importers Losing Faith in Russia"

This article centers on the ideas behind the supply and demand of oil. The article states that "with the rising demand for oil, experts suggest a significant shortage in supply of oil". **Demand** is the amount of some good or service, which an individual household consumer is willing and able to buy per period of time. In this case, although "raw" oil itself is not directly consumed by households, its byproducts such as petrol are. Certainly throughout time, the quantity demanded for oil has grown. **Supply** can be described as the quantity producers are willing and able to sell at a given price. In the case of oil, the supply curve (in a SD diagram) will be nearly vertical due to the fact that there is a fixed amount of oil available, in the **short run**. Short run refers to the period of time in which the quantity of at least one input is fixed and the quantities of the other inputs can be varied (until greater supplies of oil are "discovered"). Furthermore, we can also conclude that the supply of oil should be price **inelastic** (a large change in price would trigger a small change in QD –*diag1*. **Price elasticity** refers to the responsiveness of QD/QS to changes in price.

The article goes to mention perhaps why oil prices are at their highest (around $70 dollars a barrel). The article lists the nuclear conflict, bad weather, and a significant oil shortage coming from Nigeria (another big oil exporter). All of these reasons are related to economic theory as they would all shift the supply

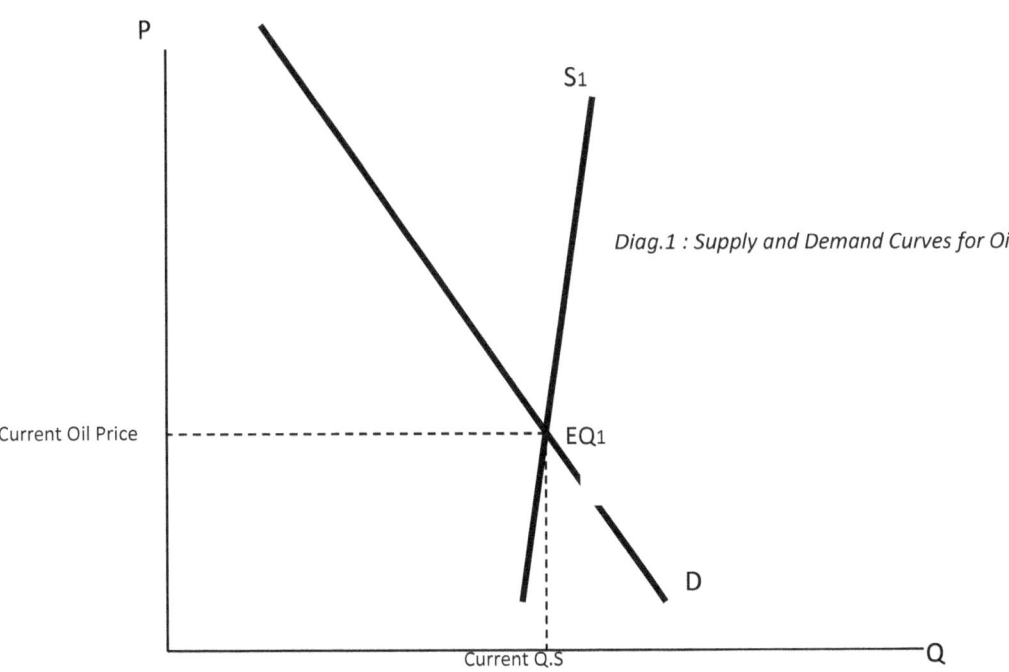

Diag.1 : Supply and Demand Curves for Oil

curve leftwards. The article refers to the fact that Russia's growth of oil output will be less than previously expected, partly due to unusually cold winters in Siberia (where most of the oil is found), thus slowing excavation and cutting supply. The breakup of two large oil producers, Sibneft and Yukos, also cost the Russian oil supply. Referring back to supply and demand diagram, if world demand rises from 84.8 million barrels a day to 85.1 million barrels of oil a day, and supply is to be 0.3 – 0.4 lower than expected (in Russia's case as much as 3% lower than expected) it can be seen in *Diag2* why oil prices would tend to rise. Supply shifts from S1 to S2 and demand from D1 to D2, as a result the **equilibrium** price would move from EQ1 to EQ2 (equilibrium means a state of equality between demand and supply).

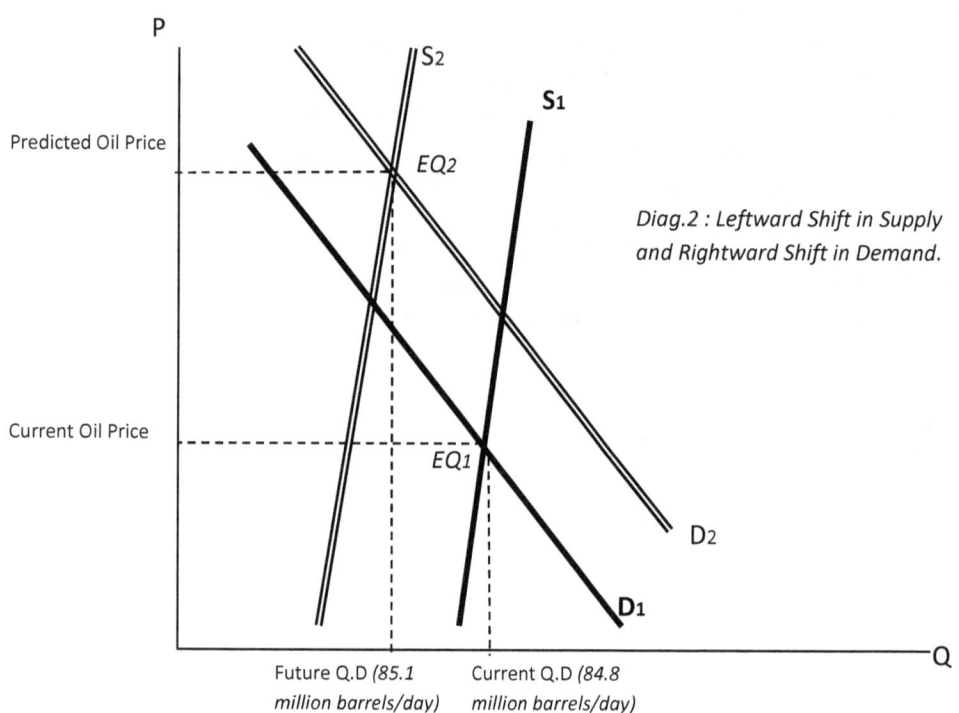

Diag.2 : Leftward Shift in Supply and Rightward Shift in Demand.

The author has at times overlooked the fact that as oil prices go up, some importers could be looking for substitutes. Currently the UK is considering increasing dependence on nuclear energy mainly due to the rising cost of oil – if alternative substitutes are cheap compared to oil, then the demand for oil could drop, represented by a shift to the right (also the more close substitutes available, the more price elastic demand will be). Importing countries could research in alternatives because oil has become such an important primary **commodity** (materials in their raw/unprocessed state). Plastic, motor, and many other industries rely heavily on the price of oil. The author unambiguously assumes that demand will keep rising because if price does rise by so much, there should be a fall in quantity demanded, and alternatives will become more viable. Also the author fails to mention who gains and who loses from these higher oil prices. Higher oil prices hurt consumers but producers/suppliers gain, so even though it still may be economically optimal, it can be argued that its inequitable since oil is a commodity and people should get its benefits at a reasonable price (the market mechanism may be working but redistribution of profits could perhaps result in greater equity in the society as a whole).

Although the author is correct to recognize the effect of depleting oil supplies, he has omitted the idea that technological advances and developments could lead to easier excavation of oil, not to mention the discovery of new reserves (both would increase supply). Moreover, the article comes from a Russian business newspaper owned by oil tycoon Boris Berezovsky, who also has strong links to the government and which is why one should question Russia's pessimistic claims about future oil supply.

In general, it is hard enough to foresee future demand or supply figures but nonetheless the author provides a good summary of the current situation with regards to the oil market.

3. 'Venezuela Inflation to End 2006 at 16%, Above Target'

This article deals with several macroeconomic concepts, notably inflation. **Inflation** is a constant rise in prices over a given time period. The article states that "Venezuelan inflation will accelerate" because of "surges in government spending" due to "record oil income" (Venezuela's oil is nationalized) and by President Chavez granting "tax reductions". The diagram below shows how rises in government spending, which is part of **aggregate demand** (defined as the total demand for an economy's goods and services), will shift the AD curve out and to the right when near or at **full employment** (AD_1 to AD_2), resulting in an increase in output from Y_1 to Y_2 and in inflation from P_1 to P_2 since aggregate supply becomes vertical. Full employment is when everyone who wants work and is willing to work at the market wage is in work. The inflation mentioned in the article is an example of **demand-pull inflation** (when total demand for goods and services is greater than supply at current prices).

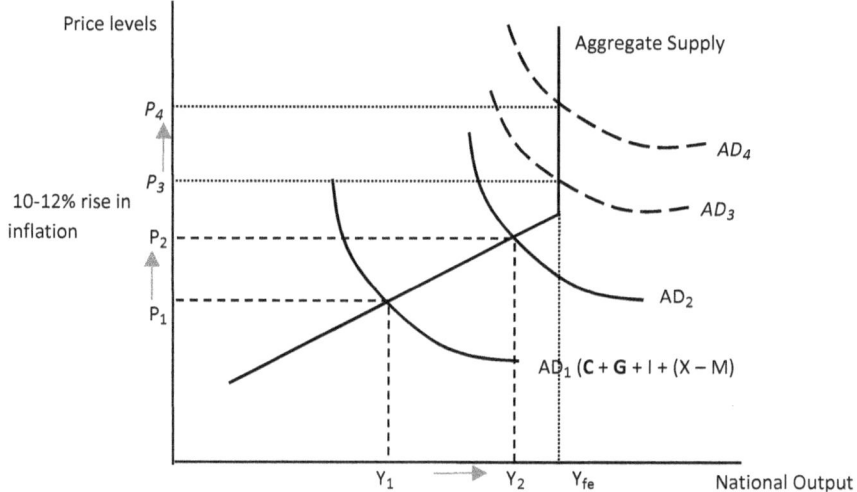

When economist Enrique Alvarez explains that if local industries were running at full capacity then it would "worsen the inflationary front in Venezuela", he is explaining that the consequences of the inflation will not be as severe, if the economy is below full employment. If the economy is at full employment, then as AD_3 grows to AD_4 there is no increase in output, but only prices. Prices still rise from P_3 to P_4 but national output remains the same, therefore there is arguably no positive effect from the inflation.

Increased government spending aside, the diagram shows how "faster economic growth" and the "inability of local manufacturers to cope with rising consumer demand" are pushing up the prices. This means an increase in consumption which shifts the AD curve to the right. When the author claims that President Chavez's plans to "grant tax reductions" will "spur inflation further", one should be careful. If tax reductions generate an equal cut in government spending, increased consumer spending will depend on the marginal propensity to consume. If MPC is less than one (if marginal propensity to save is positive), aggregate demand will decrease. The **MPC** (MPS) is the ratio of the change in consumption (saving) to the change in disposable income.

In the article, central bank president Gaston Parra mentions that policymakers aim to use a "combination of measures in the **monetary** and real spheres" to "combat inflation". Monetarists believe the link between money and aggregate demand is very strong, and if the economy is at or near full employment, like in Venezuela, growth in the money supply will lead to inflation. Measures mentioned include keeping the "currency fixed against the dollar" thereby indirectly 'importing' low inflation and credibility from the USA. "Soaking up excess cash in the system" can be done by offering higher interest rates and increasing saving. This way the public will spend less, and the cost of borrowing for businesses increases (due to an increase in interest rates) and thus reduces investment (decrease in AD).

Clearly there is a lack of "policy coordination between the government and the central bank", and as the article states - "that's where the failure to control inflation lies". From the wording of the article, it seems evident that the central bank does have some autonomy, and its main objective is inflation targeting. Although one could guess that political pressures on the central bankers are strong, this attempt to give the central bank independence is commendable, mimicking the setup in the UK, EU and USA. Independence is primarily given to solve the problem of time-inconsistency.

The argument is that if a government promises to reduce inflation to levels below those compatible with the **natural rate of unemployment** (the rate when the economy is at full employment and the labour market clears), rational public will not believe this, as the government will try to increase employment nearing re-elections and temporarily rising inflation. However, although the time-inconsistency is reduced through an independent central bank, another problem of policy coordination arises. Reading the article, it seems that the government and the central bank are playing a tug-of-war, one trying to curb inflation, while the other tries to increase employment.

The article demonstrates that an independent central bank will not be as effective at curtailing inflation as it should be if fiscal policy is counteracting monetary policy. Policy coordination is one of many aspects of which President Chavez should be reminded.

4. "Families face shock 20% rise in heating bills as gas giant's cash in on Big Freeze"

In the UK there has been a rise in prices for energy being supplied to the population. After falls in wholesale prices for the supply of energy the 'Big Six' oligopolistic energy suppliers failed to pass this on to the customers. However, after the coldest winter in 30 years, inelastic demand for energy increased, leaving the companies with windfall profits. Prices were still not reduced leading to higher bills.

Collusive oligopolies are firms in oligopolistic markets that conduct price-fixing and other uncompetitive practices. The market will act like a monopoly (graph-1.1), a type of market failure. There is formal collusion where companies price-fix formally and tacit collusion where companies charge similar prices without formal collusion. This is done to make abnormal profits since the marginal revenue and marginal cost meet at Q where it is not allocatively or efficient, to control the market.

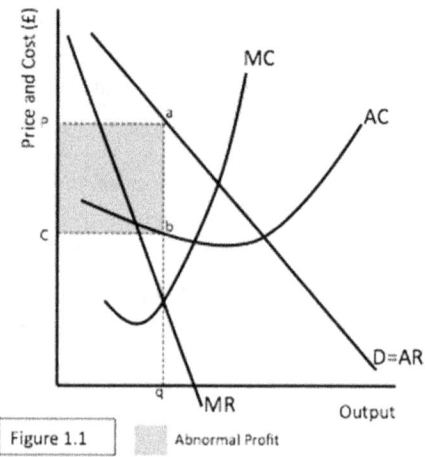

Figure 1.1 — Abnormal Profit

With a drop in prices of supply by 60% (D to D_1 on 1.2) to suppliers since 2008, the failed to pass this on and the consumer surplus should have increased, though having done this by less than 10% (£300 to p*), the 'Big Six' reaped profits when the demand for oil shot up after the coldest winter in 30 years. The average energy bills increased from £300 to £360 in a year. Subsequently, the suppliers were making profits of £846million.

With a tacit collusive oligopoly, 'Big Six' energy companies were acting like a monopoly. The problem was that in addition to not sharing the drop in supply price and earning profits from the Big Freeze, not enough energy was being supplied to bring the price back to normal; the article says that the energy being released is two years old. This imperfect competition and consumer exploitation can be seen as an example of market failure where the social marginal benefit and cost don't equate but profits are maximised at Q where marginal costs are equal to marginal revenue driving the prices up. This reduces the social and private surpluses.

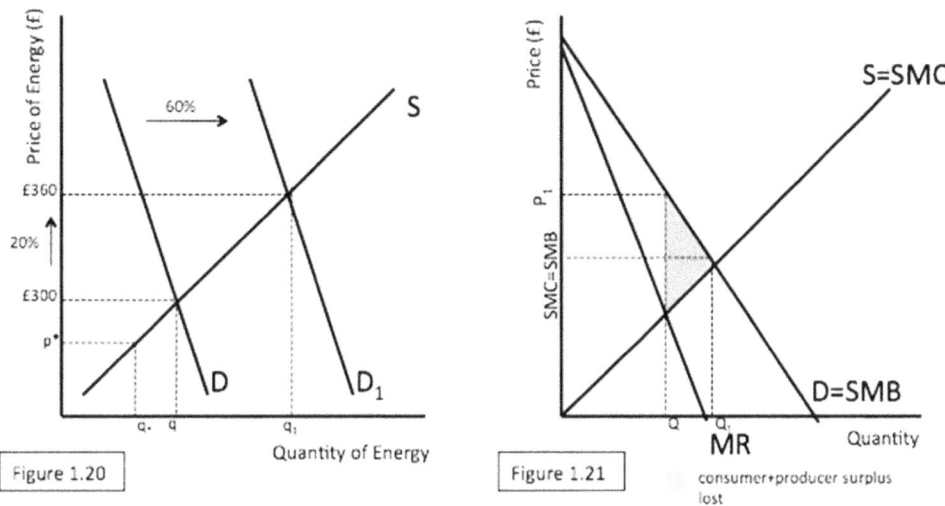

Figure 1.20

Figure 1.21

consumer+producer surplus lost

Setting a maximum price on energy could be a solution by the government. Implementing a maximum price (P_{Max}) on the cost of energy, this would reduce the price the consumers would have to pay and lower the consumer surplus; this would then exploit the consumers less. To bring the supply up, the government could encourage the release of energy (S to S_1) to supply the population and get rid of the excess demand, since the current energy is two years old. This in turn would help the high demand and bring the price back to equilibrium (P_e to P_{Max}).

Also, if the government created a stake in the energy market, they could provide an alternative source of energy. If this were not possible buffer stocks of the energy could be bought up to be released and further shift the supply of energy.

It was also mentioned in the article that the government did urge for a windfall tax on the profits made by the 'Big Six' during the Big Freeze. This money would then fund an insulation scheme that is needed.

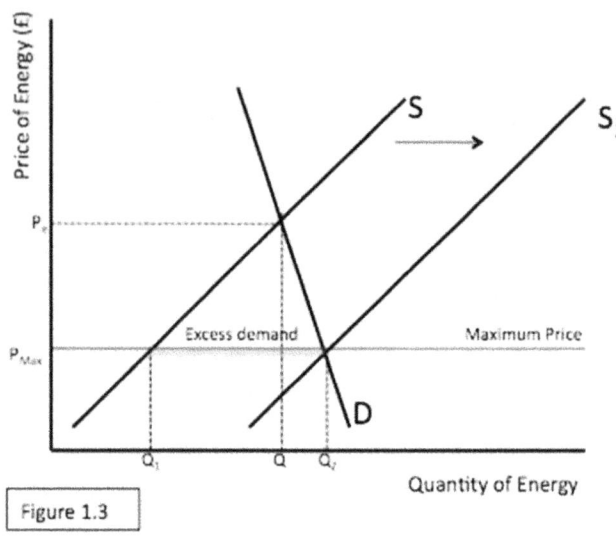

Figure 1.3

Setting a maximum price, the government will force the firms to increase energy supplies from previous stocks; this increased supply would drop the price and subsequently increase the consumer surplus so that the original drop in prices would be taxed. The limitations with this solution would be that if firms decide to release current stocks, there might be a shortage in the future as most energy sources are finite resources.

Government stake in the market would prove to be a solution since prices would be decided by the government and would not exploit the consumers. Though this might lead to administrative costs to the government in creating a new plan. In addition, political pressure that more equality and options are needed in the industry may come about.

The windfall tax that the government and unions called for, going to a £500million per annum (over 10-years) home insulation scheme from the abnormal profits earned by the firms. The oil and energy companies were meant to pay for the plan; this way the high bills of the consumers have a positive effect on the community rather than the firms. This solution seems to be the choice the UK wants to make and would have a better effect on the community.

5. 'India raises rates to rein in inflation'

High inflation rates in India during the recovery of the global recession have led the Reserve Bank of India to apply a stringent monetary policy of increasing interest rates to tackle the problem. The article discusses the effects these will have on the recovering economy.

Interest rates are defined as the cost of borrowing and the return on saving. They are used as a demand-side monetary policy to achieve economic objectives relating to a change in inflation. Demand-pull inflation is inflation caused by increasing aggregate demand in the economy.

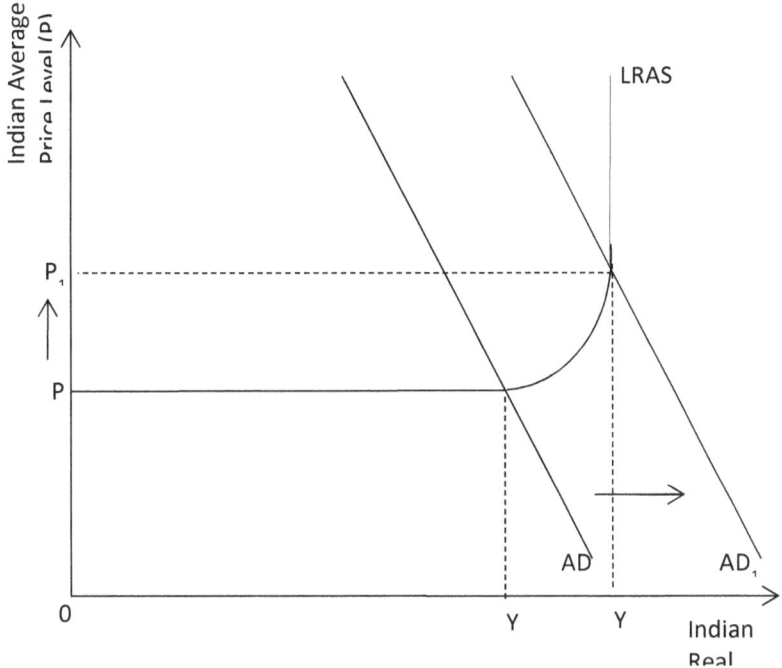

Above we can see how inflation rose during both international and domestic recovery phase of the business cycle, **"The central bank has been encouraged by a robust international outlook and a consolidated recovery in the domestic economy."** As a result the economy is approaching full employment on a Keynesian model. There is demand-pull inflation as consumers regain their confidence and increase spending (AD to AD_1) in a climate where suppliers have a lowered output due to recent recession. Average price level (P to P1) will increase as a result. In order to avoid this rising inflation the Indian government chose to use a demand-side policy to decrease the growing level of aggregate demand. Higher nominal interest rates reduce borrowing, which leads to lower demand. Since the interest rates have increased five times this year we can see that there is an attempt to find the right rate, this is known as overshooting and undershooting. The industrial production has **"bounced back"** and the agricultural industry is said to mirror this after heavy monsoon rains. Supply (SRAS to $SRAS_1$) will increase in the short run, thus further reducing inflation (P to P_1). Also, as food is a big component of the 'basket of goods', when inflation is measured it will be less so.

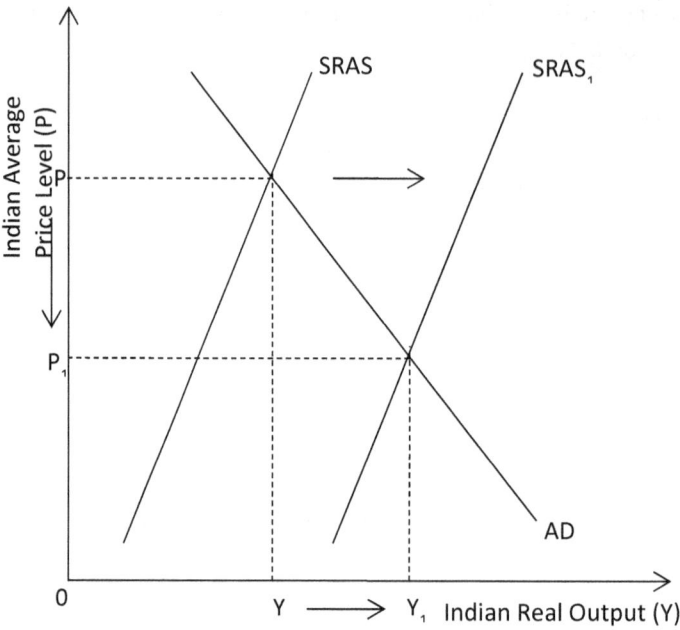

Despite this being true in the long run there are many adverse problems to increasing interest rates on such a drastic level in the short run.

With such high inflation rates the rate of investment is likely to suffer possibly hindering the supply in the economy. Business lobby groups gave a **"warning that higher interest rates would choke off investment"**. This is because the source of the funding from investments comes from borrowing. With higher interest rates (i to i_1) borrowing will decrease and so will inflation as a result (I to I_1). Since investment is the addition of capital stock in an economy and usually benefits and increases output, the reduction of its level might lead to supply falling short. This in turn would not help reduce the level of inflation. Although, seeing as this is the last increase in interest rates and during the recovery, national income and confidence are bound to increase as a result. This might put pressure on the existing capacity of the firms and encourage them to invest in the long run.

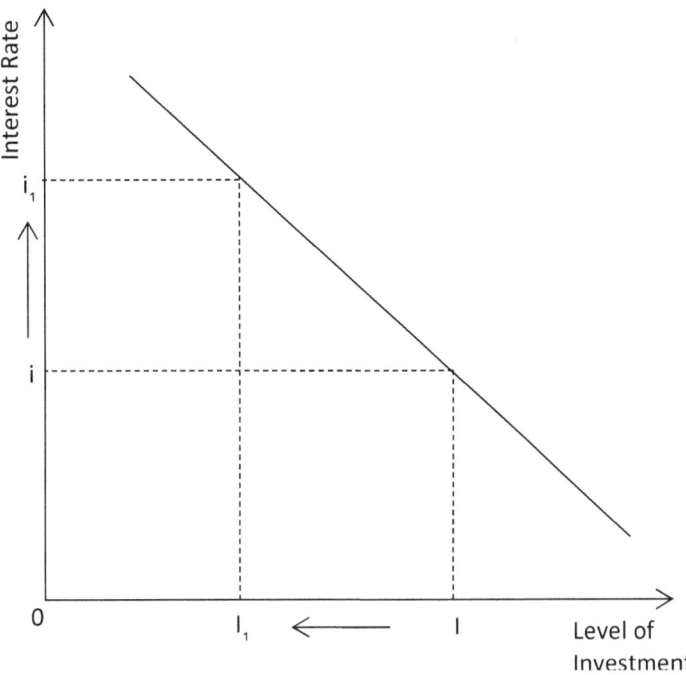

Another problem in increasing the rate briefly mentioned in the article by Mr. Chakraborty, is that the inflation of asset prices would actually rise. Assets in this case are usually real estate, bonds, derivatives, shares, all of which can be invested in through capital flows, though these would come from foreign countries. Since other countries would have relatively lower interest rates than India, saving with such a high interest rate would yield good returns. An increase in demand would drive the price up leading to inflation in this sector of the economy.

A fiscal policy with the same goal, to abate disposable income, would be increased direct taxation. This type of taxation is deemed 'unavoidable tax' and therefore it would ensure that every one if affected. Though the unfavourable fiscal policies would leave greater room for slower growth and higher unemployment due to its rate of leakages.

India is recovering at the same time as tackling high inflation. In increasing its interest rates the inflation will be reduced in the short run, with the help of growing agriculture and industrial production. Although the effects of the fifth interest rate increase this year, as a result of finding a target through overshooting and undershooting, has had an adverse effect on investment and inflations in some sectors. Since this is the last increase an eye has to be kept to make sure the balance is not lost. To keep this, different monetary policies could be used to reduce disposable income and reduce the aggregate demand.

6. 'US hits China Pipes with Tariffs'

The article discusses the problem and action taken in the United States after China reportedly **"sold OCTG (oil country tubular goods) in the United States at prices ranging from zero to 99.14% less than normal value."** This dumping on the part of the Chinese prompted the US to impose **"anti-dumping tariffs of up to 99% on imports."**

Dumping is defined as the selling of a commodity by a country at a lower price than its production cost to another country, usually brought about from a surplus of the good. A way countries protect themselves from this is by setting up tariffs, which are defined as tax on imports as a result of which the domestic price is increased, as is domestic production. Domestic consumption and volume of imports are reduced on the other hand.

The problem American OTGC manufacturers face is that China is selling large amounts of tubular goods at a lower price than the production price. In the diagram below we can see that Chinese tubular goods are sold at P (dumping) where the amount of imports consumed is Q_1-Q_4. This is moved from Q_2-Q_3 when the price was at P (world) and there was no dumping. The fact that American consumers have a reduced price than the rest of the world is advantageous. Although the problem with dumping is that domestic production, which was originally 0-Q_2 moved to 0-Q_1, is undermined and reduced as a result of a higher amount of imports.

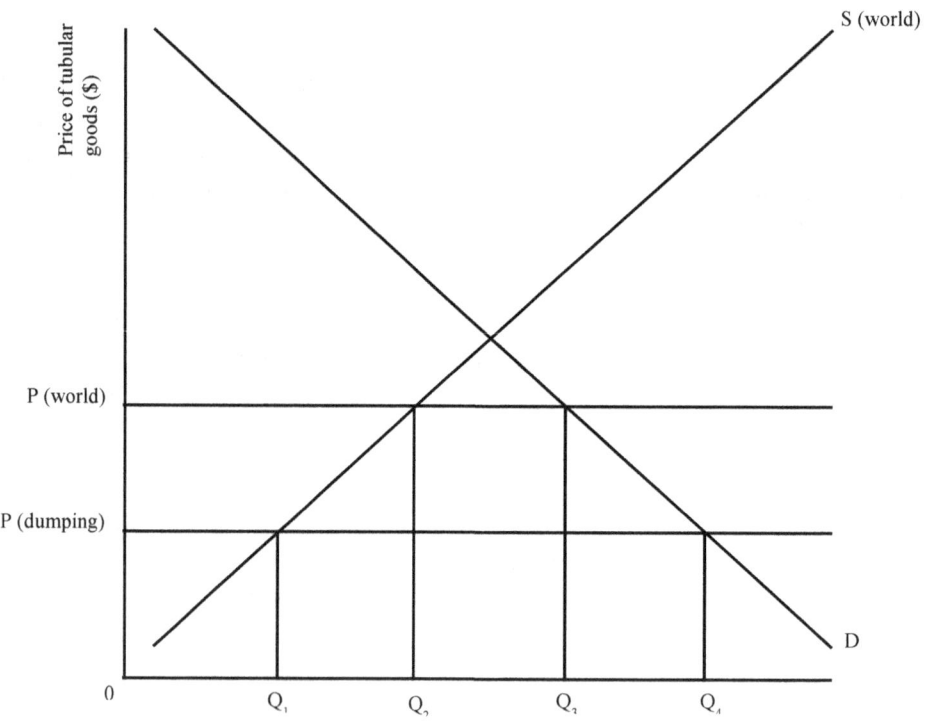

What the American government did to protect themselves was to introduce a tariff on the tubular imports. The effect it had can be represented on the graph below. This protectionism measure will push the S (World) upwards and become P (World) + tariff or P_w + tariff. This will reduce the demand from Q_2 to Q_3 and the amount of imports from Q_1-Q_2 to Q_2-Q_3. This protectionist measure ensures that domestic employment and production are not reduced or harmed further as there are less imports or more expensive imports on the domestic market. Some smaller firms or firms in decline might not be able to compete with the foreign imports and this would then lead to structural unemployment in this tubular goods industry. Setting this tariff in this case would protect the economy from low-cost labour. In China the costs of labour are much lower selling at a lower price would also reduce the domestic production.

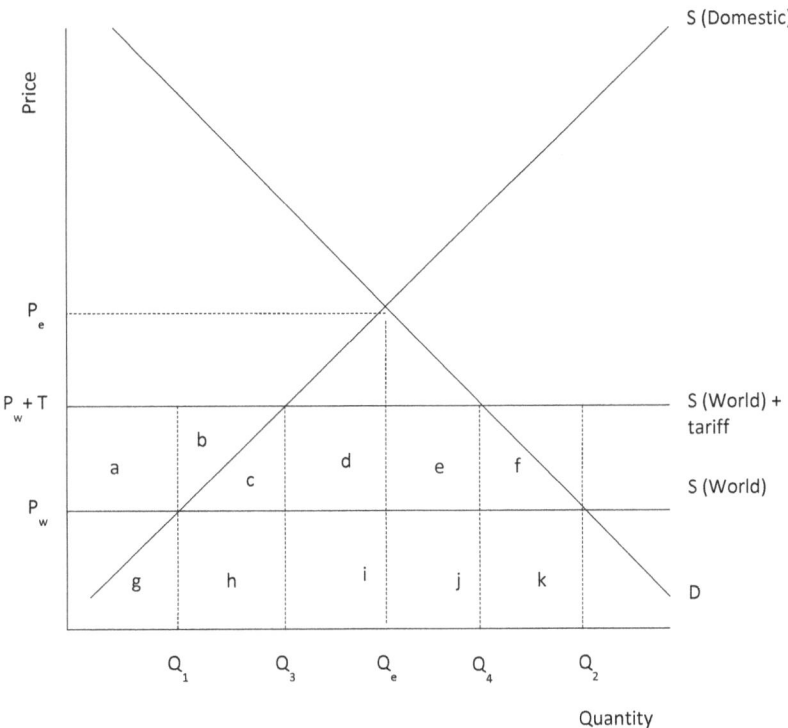

The initial problem as mentioned in the article is that **"Beijing has filed a World Trade Organisation challenge to US anti-dumping duties on certain types of steel pipes"**. It is hard to actually determine if a country is dumping or not, and if China was actually aiming to dump there might be a retaliation and further degradation in relations between the two countries. In this period of reconciliation between the two nations a trade-war in the sector could arise.

The amount of demand for tubular goods in the US might also affect the effect the tariff has in protecting against the Chinese dumping. If the tubular goods had an elastic demand there would be a higher effect from the tariffs. The more inelastic the demand is the lower effect it will have on the tubular goods. When goods are elastic the number of imports is larger and the market is more dependent on them. Either way there will need to be an increase in domestic production as a result of reduced imports. Due to the reduced competition this might cause a deficiency in the efficiency of the domestic producers.

Other options the American government could take would be setting a quota on the tubular goods. The effect this would have is represented on the graph below. This measure would put a limit on the price of a good (P quota) and would shift the domestic supply curve outwards. Q_1 would then move to Q_2 showing that the domestic production would have to increase. The problem with this situation is that it could still allow room for dumping, in that Chinese producers might still sell their products at a lower price.

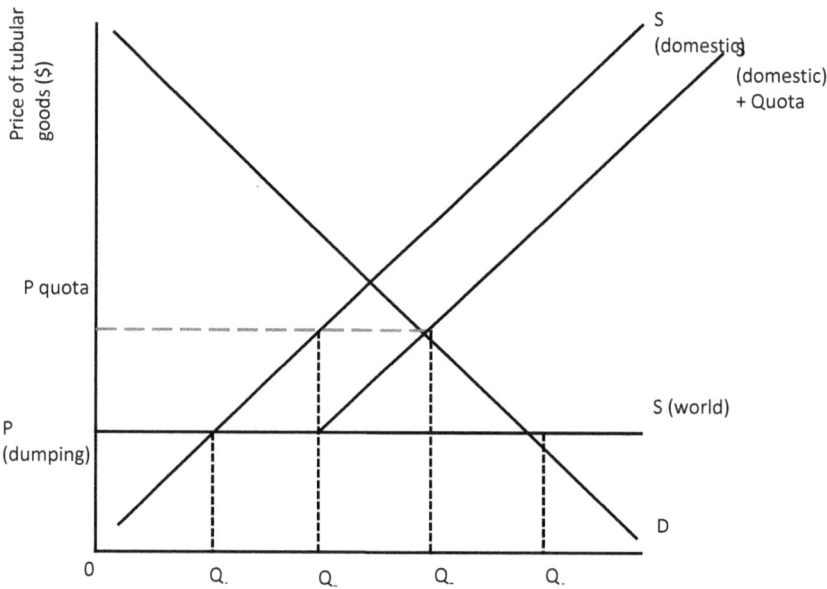

The American government could always appeal to the WTO and prove that the Chinese are dumping. Although if this is the case the implementation of a tariff would have to ensure that domestic workers are working efficiently and may need support from the government in the early stages of this change.

7. "Where is Switzerland's Cheapest Place to Live?"

Demand, supply and elasticity are basic economic concepts that when applied to different markets can help governments and individuals make informed decisions about things as basic as where to live and how to collect taxes.

Recently, Credit Suisse conducted a survey and determined that Switzerland's most expensive canton is Geneva, while the cheapest place to live is Appenzell Inner Rhodes, (AIR)

Demand is a curve showing the various amounts of a product consumers want and can purchase at different prices during a specific period of time. Supply is a curve showing the different amounts of a product suppliers are willing to provide at different prices. Equilibrium price and quantity are determined by the intersection of demand and supply. Price elasticity of demand (PED) indicates the responsiveness of consumers to a change in price, and is reflected in the relative slope of demand.

In the graph below, the markets for housing in Geneva and AIR are shown.

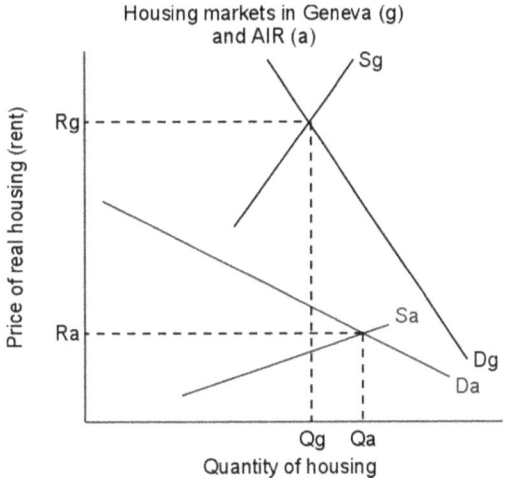

Demand for housing in Geneva (Dg), is high because of the many employment opportunities there. In addition, Geneva's scarce land means supply of housing is low, resulting in a high equilibrium rent (Rg). Demand for housing in Geneva is inelastic, since renters in Geneva are less responsive to changes in rent compared to AIR, perhaps due to the perceived necessity of living close to their work.

Demand for housing in AIR (Da) is low, but supply is high due to the abundance of land. AIR is a rural canton with few jobs, therefore fewer people are willing and able to live there than in Geneva. Since living in the countryside is not a necessity, demand is relatively elastic, or responsive to changes in rent. The lower demand and greater supply make the AIR's equilibrium rent relatively low.

The effect of a tax on property is a shift of the supply curve to the left and in increase in rents as landowners, forced to pay the canton a share of their rental incomes, raise the rent they charge residents.

In Geneva, property taxes are high, but this has little effect on the quantity demanded.

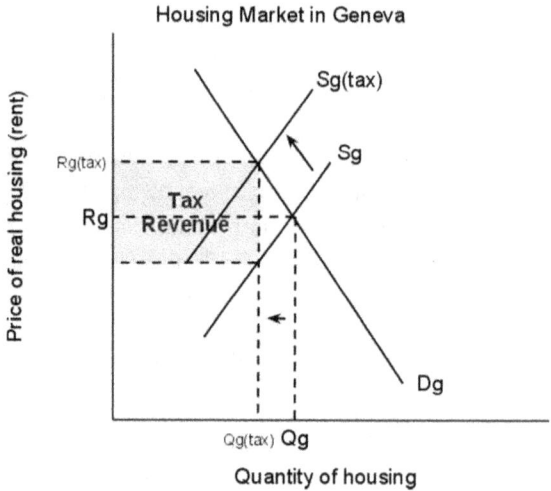

Geneva's property tax shifts the supply of housing leftwards, as fewer landlords will be willing and able to supply properties to renters when the canton taxes rental incomes. However, the decrease in quantity demanded is proportionally smaller than the increase in the price caused by the tax, since demand for housing in Geneva is highly inelastic, or unresponsive to the higher price caused by the tax.

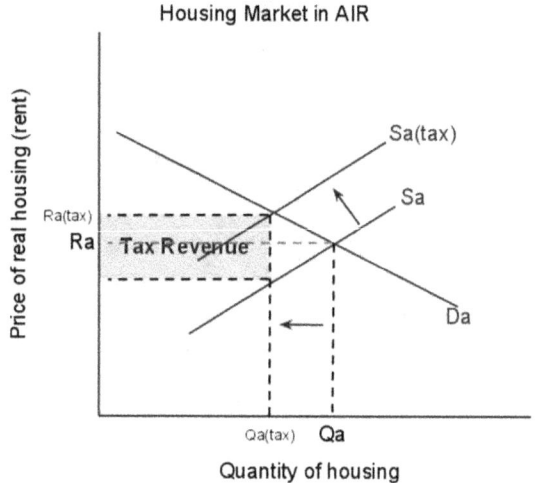

Renters in AIR are far more responsive to higher rents caused by property taxes, perhaps because living in AIR is not considered a necessity and there are more substitutes for rural cantons to live in. Renters in Geneva do not have the freedom to live in one of Switzerland's many rural cantons, and are therefore less responsive to higher rents resulting from cantonal taxes.

A tax decrease in AIR could lead to a significant increase in the number of people willing to live there, since renters are highly responsive to lower taxes. To some extent, housing in AIR and Geneva are substitutes for one another. Lower taxes in AIR would make living there more attractive, and subsequently the demand for housing in Geneva would fall putting downward pressure on rents there. People would move to AIR, attracted by lower rents, and commute to work in the cities. According to the article, this is already happening:

The disparity in the amount of disposable income… has increased the trend of people moving cantons for financial reasons… Economic necessities had led to an increase… of people moving address and opting to commute into work".

There are many determinants of demand for housing in Switzerland, the primary one being location. High rents in Geneva are explained by the high demand for and the limited supply of housing. On the other hand, residents in AIR enjoy much lower rents, due to the weak demand and abundant land. Cantons should take into consideration the PED for housing when determining their property tax levels. Raising the tax Geneva will have little effect on rentals but could create substantial tax revenue. On the other hand, reducing taxes in AIR may attract many households away from the city to the countryside, drawn by the lower rents and property taxes.

Applying the basic principles of demand, supply and elasticity to Switzerland's housing market allows households and government alike to make better decisions about where to live and how much to tax citizens.

8. 'An Impeccable Disaster: Understanding the ECB's Bond-Purchasing'

The European Central Bank (ECB) is engaging in a new form of monetary policy in which it buys government bonds directly from the Spanish and Italian governments. Essentially, the goal is to bring down the interest rates on Italian and Spanish government bonds, which should reassure private investors that Italy and Spain will be able to pay them back and thus reduce the upward pressure on interest rates in the Eurozone, a situation which threatens to reverse the already sluggish recovery from the recessions of 2008 and 2009.

Monetary policy refers to a central bank's manipulation of the money supply and interest rates, aimed at either increasing interest rates (contractionary monetary policy) or reducing interest rates (expansionary monetary policy). The ECB is currently buying government bonds from European governments, effectively increasing the supply of money in Europe with the hope that more government and private sector spending will move the Eurozone economy closer to its full employment level of output, at which workers, land and capital resources are fully employed towards the production of goods and services.

If successful, the ECB's "quantitative easing", as the new type of monetary policy is known, should bring down interest rates on government bonds and thereby reallocate loanable funds towards Italy and Spain's public and private sectors. The increase in supply of loanable funds should bring down the private interest rates available to borrows (businesses and households), making private investment more attractive.

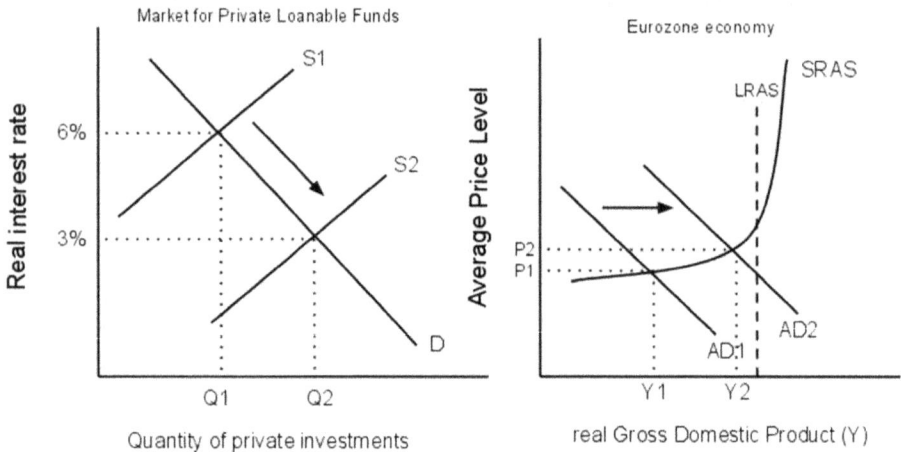

The ECB's bond purchases make it cheaper for Italy and Spain to borrow, lowering the interest rates on their bonds, restoring confidence among international investors, who may be more willing to save their money in Italy in Spain. The inflow of loanable funds into these economies (seen as an increase in the supply of loanable funds from S1 to S2) should bring down private borrowing costs (the real interest rate), encouraging more firms to invest in capital and more households to finance the consumption of durable goods, increasing aggregate demand and moving the Eurozone economy back towards its full employment level of output, from AD1 to AD2 in the graph on the right.

In certain circumstances, monetary easing like this could be inflationary, but in reality inflation is unlikely to occur given the large output gap in Europe at present (represented above as the distance between Y1 and the dotted line, signifying the full employment level of output). Any increase in aggregate demand will lead to economic growth (an increase in output), but little or no inflation due to the excess capacity of unemployed labor, land and capital resources in the European economy today.

With private sector borrowing costs increasing due to growing uncertainty over their deficits and debts, the Italian and Spanish governments will find expansionary fiscal policies (tax cuts and increased government expenditures) are unrealistic options for achieving the goal of full employment. The ECB, however, as Krugman argues, should continue to play an increasing role in the expansion of credit to cash strapped European governments, with the aim of keeping interest rates low to prevent the crowding-out of private spending that often occurs in the face of large budget deficits. Inflation, always a concern for central bankers, should be a low priority in Europe's current recessionary environment. Only when consumer and investor confidence is restored, a condition that requires low borrowing costs, will private sector spending resume and the Euro economies can begin creating jobs and increasing their output again.

In the short-term, Italy and Spain should take advantage of the ECB's bond-buying initiative, and make meaningful, productivity-enhancing investments in infrastructure, education and job training. If their economies are to grow in the future, Eurozone countries must become more competitive with the rapidly expanding economies of Asia, Eastern Europe, and elsewhere in the developing world.

In the medium-term, the Eurozone countries must demonstrate a commitment to fiscal restraint and more balanced budgets. Eliminating loopholes that allow businesses and wealthy individuals to avoid paying taxes, for example, is of utmost importance. Also, increasing the retirement age, downsizing some of the more generous social welfare programs and increasing marginal tax rates on the highest income earners would all send the message to investors that these countries are committed to fiscal discipline. Then, in time, their dependence on ECB lending will decline and private lenders will once again be willing to buy Eurozone government bonds at lower interest rates, allowing for continued growth in the private sector.

9. "Irish plastic bag tax set to rise"

This article examines Ireland's effort to increase the tax set on plastic bags in a hopeful attempt to limit the consumption of bags, thus benefiting the environment. A **tax** is money obliged by a government in return for its support and is charged upon incomes, property, or sales.

The Government's revenue, partly from taxes, is used to provide services in the economy such as education or transport. In this case, the taxes set on plastic bags are used to fund environmental projects. Since plastic bags cannot be decomposed, they cause a great deal of waste towards our environment. The Government's attempt to tax the negative externality from using these bags can limit their production, therefore producing less litter in our world. The cost of producing plastic bags is a **negative externality** which is experienced by third parties, not the producers and consumers who use them.

There are two types of taxes: indirect and direct. **Direct** taxes are taken directly from people's incomes or business's profits. However, **indirect** taxes are imposed on the supplier's goods or services. In this article, the indirect tax is set on the supplier's plastic bags. Since suppliers will produce more bags when their prices of goods rise, the supply curve is shown to be directly proportionate to price (**law of supply**). Many factors can move the supply curve but taxes shift the supply curve to the left as the cost to the firm is greater, hence supply decreases.

One type of indirect tax is a **specific tax**, similar to the one of plastic bags, has a certain set value which is paid. A specific tax therefore does not matter how much the price is on a good or service since the same extra amount is always paid. This is shown below:

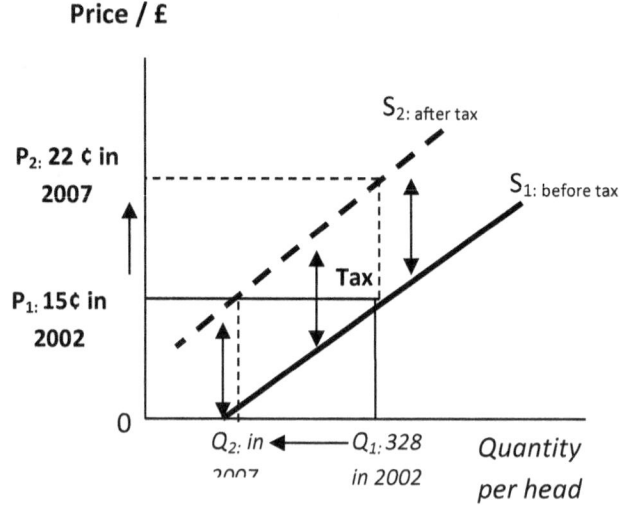

Diagram 1: Specific Tax set on the supply of retailers

A tax is a cost of production so S_1 shifts left to S_2 as the tax causes the same amount of plastic bags to increase in price. The Government tries to shift the supply curve by taxing and then resulting in a decrease in supply as retailers will now have to pay more for purchasing the bags than before. The amount of tax paid to the government is the space between the two curves, S_1 and S_2 is kept the same, disregarding the initial price, S_1. The suppliers at Q_1 who were paying 15 cents for the plastic bags now have to pay a higher price of 22 cents to buy the same amount of bags, but they are not content doing that. As a result, the suppliers will limit their supply or in effect not supply at all so theoretically their quantity decreases to Q_2. This is how a specific tax set on plastic bags can cause suppliers to limit their usage of bags in Ireland.

Economic theory suggests that if an indirect tax is set on a supplier, they try to shift the burden of the tax to the consumer by increasing the prices of their product. In this case (diagram 1) however, the tax is not being passed on as the bags are being given out freely to consumer; thus, there is no demand to shift the burden of the tax to. Personally, a better option would be to price plastic bags for consumers to alert them of the damaging effects they bring to the environment. The tax would then limit the usage by consumers and perhaps they would shift to other substitutes, preferably long-life or reusable bags which would be cheaper.

After the tax was imposed in 2002, the amount of bags used decreased from 328 to 21 per head but then it boosted to 30 bags in 2006. A reason for this wasn't stated in the article. However, economic theory suggests that since plastic bags might be considered as a necessity for retailers, the tax will not have a great affect over the long term – longer than a year – as suppliers will continue to buy these bags. An adding factor to the 2006 increase of bag usage might be the complaints suppliers received from consumers about not having grocery bags for their groceries. Economic theory states discontented consumers contribute to the firm's failure; hence suppliers have begun using bags again since they couldn't afford to lose customers. Consequently, to maintain the prevention of the usage of bags in order to benefit the environment, the Government has raised the tax again.

10. "DVD chain sounds the death knell for rentals market"

The piece examines the declining demand of ChoicesUK's rental DVDs because of increasing substitutes available. **Demand** is the ability and willingness of consumers to purchases goods and services over a certain amount of time.

One of the main causes of changes in quantity demand is price. According to economic theory, the quantity of consumers who are willing to rent DVDs at a cheaper price will be more than the quantity of consumers who are willing to rent at a more expensive price. Hence, the **law of demand** states that a higher quantity of consumers will demand a product at a lower price assuming *ceterus parabus* – all other factors remain constant. Thus, the relationship between demand and price is inversely proportional as seen in *diagram 1* below with the curve labeled D_1. The **demand curve** shows the quantity that consumers are willing and able to rent at each price (*cet. par*).

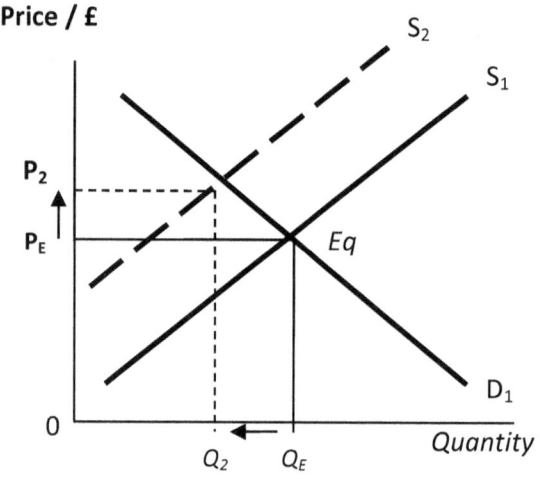

Diagram 1: The supply and demand curves for DVD rentals

The **supply** of rentals is the quantity producers are able and willing to supply at a given price. According to the **law of supply**, an increase in price will usually lead to an increase in the quantity supplied and so they are directly proportional. The supply of rentals is represented above by the line S_1. When supply equals demand **equilibrium** exists at *Eq*. There is no mention of supply in the article – except for the fact that ChiocesUK decided to diversify their product range by selling computer games. Since ChiocesUK increased their supply of computer games, more resources will be focused on providing computer games, so then their supply of DVD rentals will decrease. This is shown through the shift to the left of the supply line from S_1 to S_2 on diagram 1. According to economic theory, the increase of substitute supply such as computer games will decrease demand of DVD rentals from Q_1 to Q_2.

In the article it states that there are determinants, other than price, which are affecting the demand of the products at ChiocesUK. Firstly, due to global warming, the UK has become much warmer during the year. People have become eager to go out and enjoy the warmth, rather than stay home and watch films. Another cause of the declining demand for DVDs is the rapid changes in technology. Nowadays, teenagers would rather illegally download free pirated movies off the internet than pay to rent one. Other substitutes are renting DVDs from online rentals as it is easier to access. In addition, the price of substitute products has gone down as huge retailers, Virgin and HMV, have decreased their prices drastically that ChoicesUK appears too expensive. This is some evidence of economic theory that as the price of substitute's decreases, the demand of a product will decrease as consumers shift to buying the cheaper good.

Each of these factors affects the demand curve by shifting it to the left as seen below:

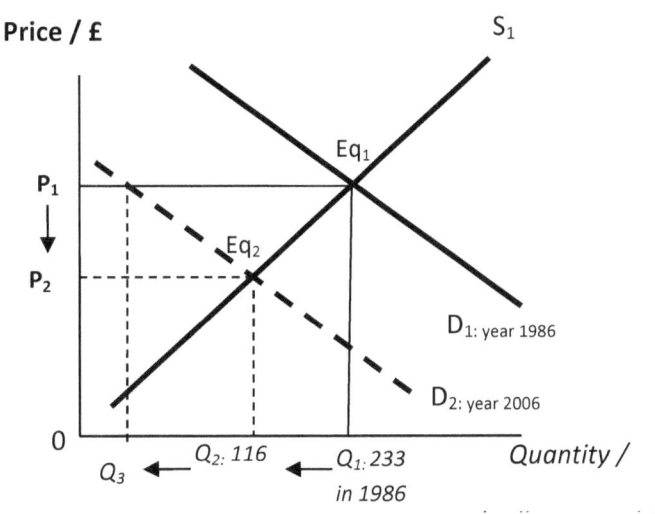

Diagram 2: The decrease in demand of rentals over time

The initial demand curve – D_1 – represents the demand of rentals in the year 1986. Q_1 is the amount of rentals consumers bought: 233 million. And P_1 is the symbolic price that the average consumers paid for the rentals. When demand equals supply **equilibrium** exists at Eq_1. In the year 2006, the demand shifts to the left to D_2 and a new equilibrium, Eq_2, is formed where the quantity of demand, Q_2, decreases to just 116 million rentals.

The article does not mention that the price of rentals has decreased over time, but economic theory suggests that if demand decreases, price must also decreases. This is shown by the new equilibrium point and the label of the new price, P_1. If ChoicesUK kept their prices at P_1 – even as the demand drastically lowered (due to the factors mentioned above) – then it in effect would lower even more because of the high price. The consumers that are still buying the rentals (without the adjustment of prices) are represented on the diagram as Q_3. Without lowering the price to adjust to low demand, economic theory suggests a greater decrease in demand. Perhaps if ChiocesUK lowered their price, consumers would then have more interest in their products.

In addition, ChoicesUK has diversified their product range with the supply of computer games which have become 40 percent of their sales. One would think that the warm weather would apply to computer games just as it does on DVD rentals. In addition, computer games could be pirated. As a result, economic theory suggests these determinants will limit the demand of computer games but actually does not.

11. "Consumer spending up as inflation eases"

After years of battling with high inflation rates, there now have been fears that the US is slowly falling into recession, however, the recent increase in consumer spending might prove otherwise. A **recession** occurs when an economy experiences a fall in GDP or the total economic activity in a country for two consecutive quarters. An economy's total spending on goods and services at a certain price over time is called the **aggregate demand** of the economy. Aggregate demand is made up of investment, consumption, government expenditure, exports and imports.

One main factor of aggregate demand is **investment**, which is the addition of capital stocks such as machinery or factories to the economy. When a firm wants to invest, they need money which they can borrow or use from their retained profits. Both of these sources are affected by **interest rates** which are the costs of borrowing money. If the cost of borrowing money is high, then investment will fall. The same will happen if firms decide to use their profits to invest: if interest rates are high, firms will prefer to save their profits in the bank. In the article, the Federal Reserve decided to enforce the Monetarist view and "cut a key interest rate by one-half point" to increase investment, which follows the economic theory of the inverse relationship between investment and interest rates. Usually, the Fed only makes changes by a quarter of a point, but in order to ensure changes in the economy they have decreased their interest rates by a larger amount.

As a result of certain population trends and a fall in interest rates, consumer spending has also increased. The article states that spending rose by 0.6% due to a "big jump in auto sales." However this recent measure taken by the Fed of lowering interest rates will allow consumers to borrow more money and purchase more durable goods such as houses or cars.

As shown on the diagram below, an increase in investment will shift the aggregate demand curve to the right. Similar to microeconomics demand, aggregate demand also has an inverse relationship with price. This will shift the initial equilibrium point Eq1 to Eq2, increasing real GDP from Q_E to Q_2 and price level from P_E to P_2. The following increase in consumer demand as well as other factors such as rising income mentioned in the article will shift the AD_2 curve to AD_3.

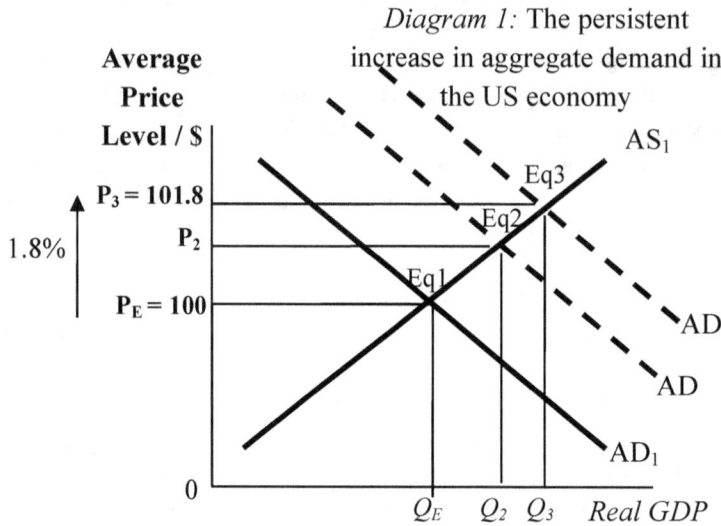

Diagram 1: The persistent increase in aggregate demand in the US economy

This persistent increase in aggregate demand will continue to increase the price level in the economy from P_E to P_2 to P_3. This is called **demand-pull inflation** since it is caused by the increasing aggregate demand of the US economy. The article states that inflation has "eased" from previous years, and so consumer spending has increased by 0.6% as the price level of goods and services will be less than they previously were. Even though consumption has increased, investment has been extremely low for the past 16 years due to "a serious credit crunch" and so lowering interest rates will not have a great effect on investment. There has also been a loss of 4,000 jobs which means that less people can afford to spend what they used to, limiting the GDP in the economy. Certainly, these two factors counter balance the rise in consumer expenditure, which shows how inflation has "eased" rather than increased. But economic theory suggests that if several determinants of demand persistently increase, such as investment and consumer expenditure, then this will shift the aggregate demand to the right, causing a rise in price level. This means that by lowering interest rates, inflation will rise eventually – if not now – which goes against the initial inflation problem the Fed is battling against.

Indeed we should be skeptical about the way the Fed has measured the inflation rate. The **core price** uses certain prices of goods and services as indicators to measure inflation. Usually these core prices include the main consumption goods and services in an economy; however, they have excluded energy and food. These two goods should be some of the primary goods used to measure inflation. Interestingly enough, if the Fed had taken into account these factors in their core price, inflation may have risen, showing that the measure of core inflation is lacking accuracy.

12. "China raises export tariffs on steel to reduce trade surplus"

Due to the recent rapid growth in China and demands from the U.S. and Europe, China is forced to act on its cheap **exports** – the sale of goods and services to buyers from foreign countries. By acting on its exports China can protect itself from inflation and will potentially ensure protectionism for the U.S. and Europe. **Protectionism** is the imposition of trade barriers to protect incomes of domestic producers.

In consequence of China's relatively cheap exports, the U.S. and European domestic producers are suffering. China's exports are so cheap that it is being accused of **dumping** – the process of foreign (Chinese) firms selling goods at a loss to destroy domestic industries (in US and Europe). Therefore, China has recently set export tariffs on their steel and coke products – some of the products which they supply to the majority of the world. The **export tariffs** set by China is a tax set on its' domestic goods to make them more expensive and discourage foreigners to buy China's exports.

Diagram 1 shows the effects of an export tariff. The world supply, S_{w1}, is infinitely elastic as the world market is not directly affected by China's Yuan. The effect of China introducing a tax on its exports is like any indirect taxation: it affects the domestic supply line shifting it to the left from S_{D1} to S_{DT}, moving the equilibrium point from Eq1 to Eq2. Naturally, as taxes increase the cost of production, the price of exports will increase from P_E to P_2 and so the quantity of exports initially at Q_E will reduce to Q_2.

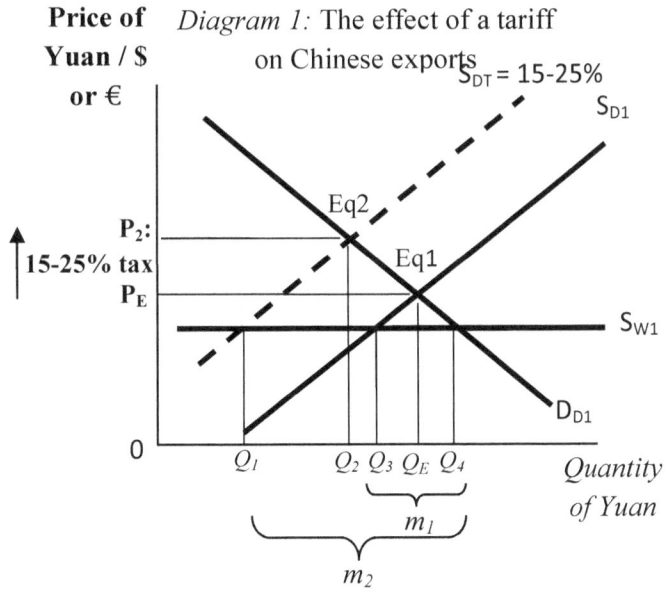

What the export tariff does is reduce Chinese exports but also indirectly increases imports into China. **Imports** are the buying of foreign goods and services. This is seen on diagram 1 as the amount of imports increases from $Q_3Q_4(m_1)$ to $Q_1Q_4(m_2)$. By implementing export tariffs, China allows the world market to be more competitive with its exports and may potentially lower China's export revenue which is rarely done in many countries.

This has not been the only measure taken in order to reduce its **trade surplus** caused by its export revenue being larger than its import expenditure. China has lowered its **import tariffs** – taxes set on foreign goods to make them more expensive and encourage consumers to switch to domestic goods and services. By lowering China's import tariff, China will now allow for cheaper imports to be bought domestically and so will enable imports to be more compatible with domestic goods.

Referring to diagram 2, the world supply S_{W1} is initially at P_1. After lowering the import tariff, the price of imports will fall to P_2 as foreign suppliers will no longer have to pay as much tax as they previously were paying to import their goods into China. Due to the law of demand, lowering the import tariff will raise the quantity of imports being bought in China from $Q_2Q_3(m_1)$ to $Q_1Q_4(m_2)$. Again, the measures taken by China are ironic as lowering import tariffs may potentially risk domestic suppliers as imports will be more competitive with domestic goods and services.

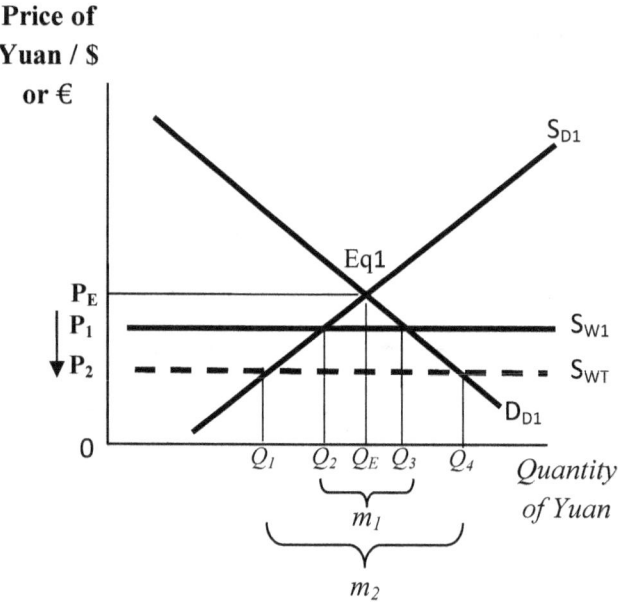

Diagram 2: The effect of cutting import tariffs in China

China's Yuan is currently pegged to the US dollar which means its currency does not reflect the demand and supply of its own currency but instead, America's. What is questionable about China's method to reduce its trade surplus is that it could have easily unpegged it's currency to the dollar, allowing for a **floating exchange rate** where China's currency is allowed to move freely according to the amount demanded and supplied of its currency. Due to its trade surplus, its currency would appreciate relative to the US's currency. Countries willing to buy exports will then require more of their currency to exchange it for the Yuan, making Chinese exports more expensive. Potentially this causes a fall in quantity demanded of exports and imports become relatively cheaper to domestic goods whose prices would rise after the Yuan's appreciation – solving its problem without impositions of tariffs. This may also help reduce Chinese inflation (the persistent increase in aggregate demand) caused by their trade surplus.

13. 'Minimum Price on Alcohol'

Over the past few years, England has seen a rapid increase in the amount of people drinking at hazardous or harmful levels. A large portion of this increase lies with the young binge drinkers and the heavy compulsive drinkers. In an attempt to halt this shocking rise in alcohol consumption, and reduce the negative effects on society, the Health Select Committee (H.S.C) and Members of Parliament have called for minimum pricing and negative advertising on alcoholic drinks.

The committee is trying to reduce the negative externalities that result from the consumption of alcohol. These externalities are negative impacts on third parties resulting from the consumption of an economic good; marginal social benefits are less than the marginal private benefits. In this case, the consumption of alcohol negatively affects health care, increases crime rates and decreases output due to employees taking days off or dying prematurely.

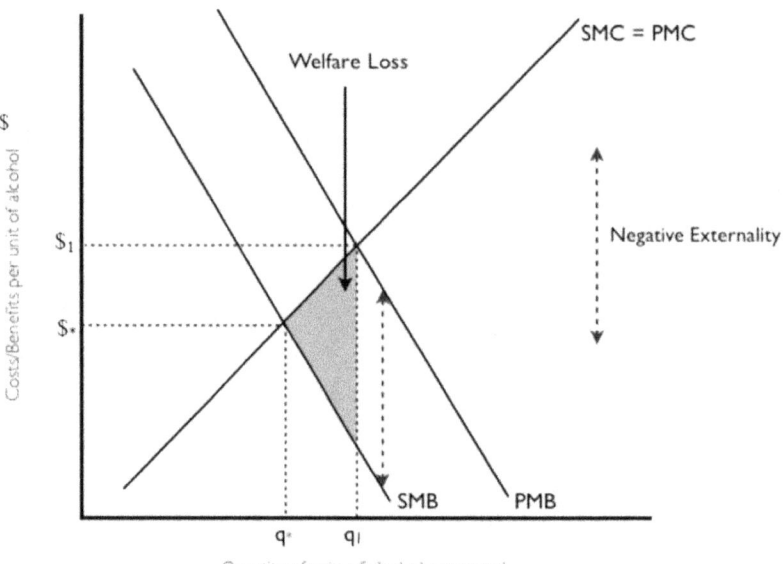

The negative externalities mentioned above characterize demerit goods like alcohol. If left to the market, scarce resources would not be allocated efficiently and these goods would be over-provided and overproduced, resulting in Market Failure.

A series of strategies proposed by the government are meant to make drinking more expensive for the excessive drinkers and binge drinkers, hopefully making it less attractive to buy alcohol, decreasing demand.

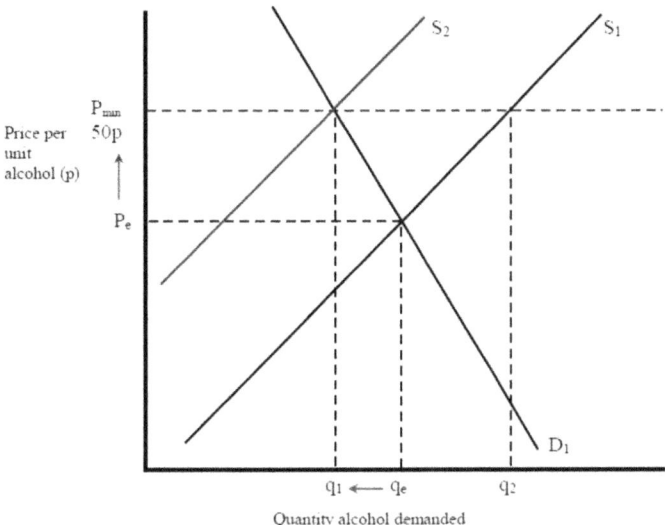

The first, and most favored solution is the introduction of a minimum price per unit of alcohol. The H.S.C "recommends a rise in the price of drinks as the most effective way of bringing down consumption and reducing the annual (death) toll of 40,000." This price, which is determined by the government, is set above equilibrium price and will discourage drinkers from buying alcohol. "A minimum price of 50p a unit could save an estimated 3000 lives each year." (Pe to Pmax)

Three main groups need to be considered when deciding on a minimum price. In order for this solution to be successful the government must assume that the demand for alcohol is elastic. Especially in the older, compulsive drinkers, alcohol is a habit-forming (inelastic) good. Therefore a minimum price might have little or no effect on this group.

Another problem is the fact that the social drinkers who drink acceptable quantities of alcohol might be affected. The article, however, disproves this by saying that "someone drinking six units (moderate consumption) of alcohol a week would pay 11p a week more than at present."

The target of a minimum price would be the young binge drinkers who favor the "cheap high strength lagers and industrial white cider." Their demand is relatively elastic since they have no steady source of income and therefore rely on cheap, strong alcohol.

Finally, a minimum price would encourage the introduction of a black-market such during the Prohibition in America during the 1920s. People would begin to brew their own alcohol which brings more dangers and negative externalities with it, exactly what the Committee is trying to reduce.

The second strategy to reduce alcohol consumption is to force companies to post compulsory health warnings on the labels of alcoholic beverages, similar to those on cigarette packets. This form of negative advertising will attempt to change people's views on alcohol and shift the demand curve to the left.

Negative advertising will make drinkers more aware of the dangers involved, but the costs of funding the advertisements may be high, especially in the long run. In the short-run, a nationwide advertising campaign over the course of a couple of months could produce the same effect, as well as limiting the costs. Also, many drinkers may be willing to accept the dangers of drinking and this solution would thereby lose its effectiveness.

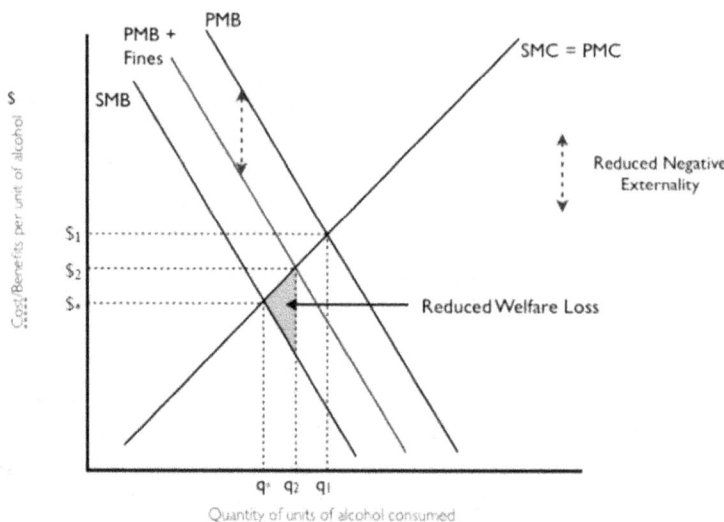

A solution not mentioned in the article could be the introduction of fines on individuals who drink excessive amounts. The money generated from these fines could then be used to finance the negative advertising and to educate young children about alcohol. The combination of fines and education would discourage the consumption of alcohol and reduce the welfare loss.

A minimum price would be the most effective solution to reduce the excessive consumption of alcohol, but not on its own. Education and negative advertising must also be implemented, and the costs of this can be covered with fines on alcohol consumption.

14. 'The Iron Ore Oligopoly'

The iron ore industry is a crucial sector in today's economy and is used to create virtually all of the world's steel. The industry itself is dominated by three major firms: The British-Australian multinational *Rio Tinto*, the Brazilian mining company *Vale,* and the world's largest mining company, *BHP Billiton.* These three firms have a combined market share of almost 70% and also "also constitute 90 per cent of the global seaborne iron ore market." This article addresses the concerns that arose with the merging of two of these three major competitors, *BHP Billiton* and *Rio Tinto*. The Australian Competition & Consumer Commission is concerned that this affiliation will result in an even greater market concentration, and "could provide a strong incentive for the majors to withhold iron ore to push up price."

Since so much of the market share is controlled by three firms, they create an *oligopoly.* This is when there are few interdependent firms in the industry, with some barriers to entry. The ACCC is trying to stop the formation of a collusive oligopoly or even a *monopoly*, which is when the market contains one firm and very high barriers to entry. Through this the dominant firm could charge *abnormal profits,* any level of profits above the minimum required for a firm to remain in an industry.

The ACCC is looking to stop the newly merged 'super-firm' and possibly *Vale,* from forming a monopoly or a collusive oligopoly. In this type of market there is less competition and the firm or firms agree to push up prices while they "actually produce less than what BHP and Rio would produce if the merger does not occur."

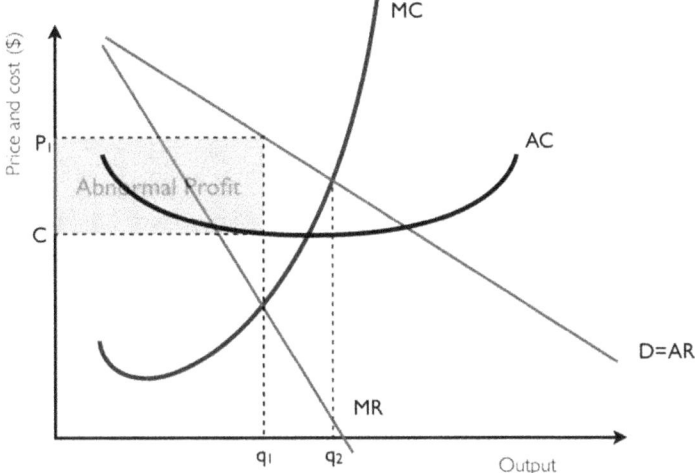

On the monopoly diagram above, we can see that in a competitive market, the firm would produce at the profit maximizing point MC = MR. This would be represented by (q_2) since in that case D=AR=MR. In a monopoly the MR is not identical to the demand curve and is actually twice as steep. Therefore supply will be restricted, and higher price charged (q_1, p_1), resulting in the abnormal profits shown.

However, if we bring economies of scale into the equation we get a completely different picture. Economies of scale occurs when any firm experiences increasing returns to scale, which means that being a large firm is advantageous.

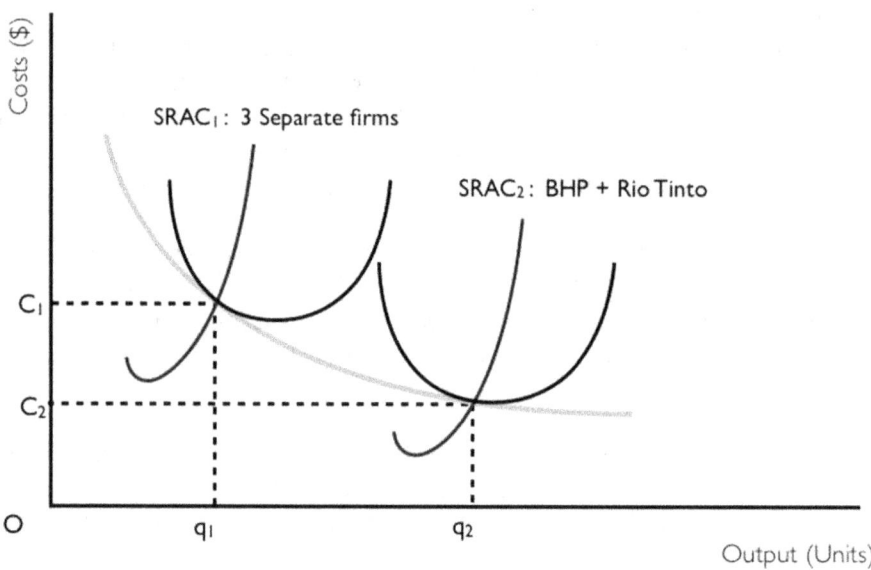

On the long-run average cost curve we can demonstrate the economies of scale. Say the three individual firms in question each have a short run average cost curve at point (q_1, C_1). But the large firm formed by the merging of *BHP* and *Rio Tinto* experiences increasing returns to scale and can therefore produce at (q_2, C_2), at a higher output and lower price. This scenario would be in the *public interest* and therefore the ACCC would not have to intervene.

The reason the ACCC is being so critical is that: "If BHP and Rio produce less than they otherwise would have, the impact on the competitive position of BlueScope (an Australian steel company) is going to be quite significant." In this case the merging would not be in the public interest. Prices of steel would force upwards, resulting in a negative impact on the public. If this happens then the ACCC proposes that: "conditions [be] put in place, to ensure the joint venture meets the requirement of the ACCC." These conditions could come in the form of a maximum price or monitoring by the Australian anti-trust authorities.

There are problems with this though. It is difficult for governments to judge on the type and strictness of regulation. Large firms also have influence over government parties, and these two factors could impair firms from making normal profits even if they are not colluding, or render the regulations useless.

A similar solution is a limit on the mining rights per company. This would stop large companies from buying up all the rights, and give smaller firms the opportunity to compete. Again the countries or the regulators need to make sure they are not limiting the (natural) growth of the large firms.

Governments and regulators must first determine whether the joint venture of *BHP* and *Rio Tinto* is in the public interest. The merging could be advantageous to consumers if the industry experiences economies of scale. However, if this not the case, then conditions that do not excessively restrict the firm's profits must be implemented.

15. 'Europe's Inflationary Concern'

As Europe and the rest of the world are facing "debt concerns and fiscal austerity measures," China's economy is experiencing a boom. Since March 2009, the Chinese growth rate has been increasing by one percent per quarter, and in March 2010 the GDP growth rate hit a "19-month high" of 12 percent. One of the biggest consequences that China is experiencing due to these high growth rates is rising inflation. Economists fear that price levels will continue to rise and are advising the Chinese central bank to raise interest rates to counter this.

Inflation, which is a persistent increase in the average price levels of an economy over a period of time is not necessarily undesirable. Low rates of inflation, also known as creeping inflation are acceptable and this is what countries usually aim for. High inflation, such as the "3.1 percent" increase in China, negatively affects many aspects of the economy such as savings, purchasing power and international competitiveness.

The major concern mentioned in the article is that the already high inflation rates could be pushed upwards even more if "Chinese workers are successful in their efforts to get higher wages." The economists are essentially warning China that they could find themselves in an inflationary spiral if they do not act. An inflationary spiral occurs when demand-pull and cost-push inflation combine to drive inflation sky-high. The Chinese economy is already overheating, meaning Aggregate Demand is moving outwards (AD1 to AD2). If wages were to increase, then this would increase the costs to firms, shifting Aggregate Supply to the left (AS1 to AS2). Finally, increased wages might give households the illusion that they have increased spending power, and will push Aggregate Demand (AD) to the right again (AD2 to AD3). This upward spiral is represented in the diagram below.

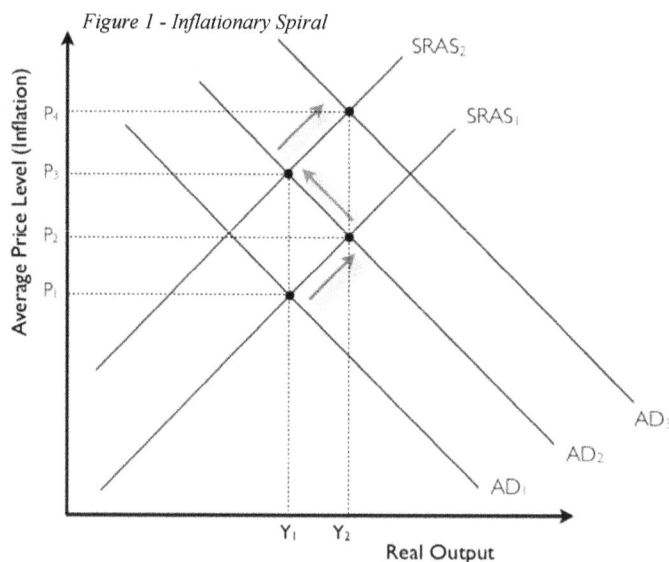

Figure 1 - Inflationary Spiral

The article states that, "The Chinese authorities would have to intensify their efforts to tame the pace of growth and unwanted side effect of inflation." The main strategy proposed by the economists to bring down the inflation, is an increase in interest rates. This type of *monetary policy* is the most effective method to bring down economic activity when an economy is overheating. Increasing the interest rates will increase the cost of borrowing money, making saving money more attractive for consumers. Also, since borrowed money is usually used for larger purchases, households might find these purchases more expensive when interest rates are high and therefore postpone them. Interest rates also determine the cost of people's mortgages, and so consumers will have less disposable income as interest rates are increased.

Yet there are a few consequences that the Chinese government and central bank must consider before increasing the target interest rates. First, the possible tradeoff between inflation and unemployment. China can try to slow the economy down by using deflationary monetary policy, but this would cause an increase in unemployment at the same time; it must find an acceptable relationship between inflation and unemployment. This tradeoff can be shown using the Phillips Curve.

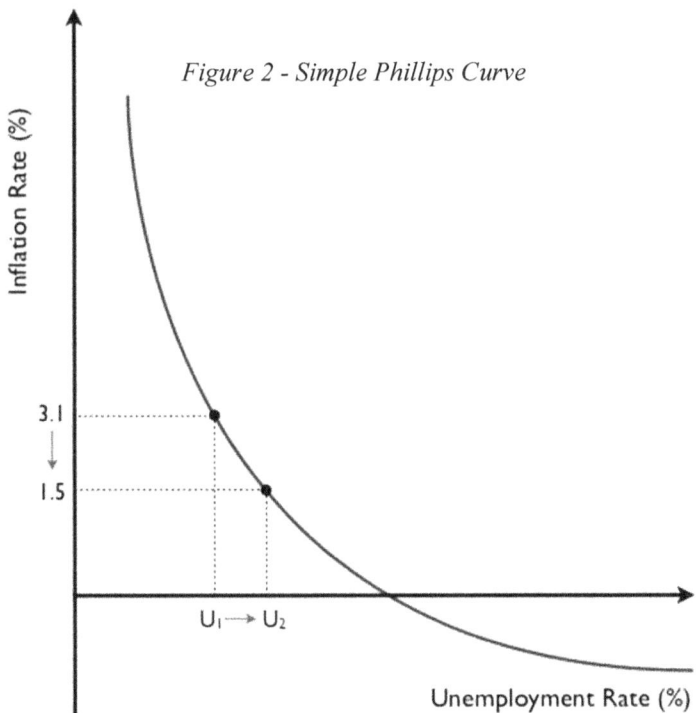

Figure 2 - Simple Phillips Curve

Another problem the central bank could face is the time lag between when they set the interest rate and when it begins to affect the economy. Although changing interest rates is a fairly accurate macroeconomic tool compared to fiscal policy, there is still a chance of under- or overshooting. If we also take into account the multiplier effect, where an initial change in AD leads to a greater final effect on national income, there is a potential risk of overshooting and creating deflation.

Bringing down aggregate demand through interest rates would be a step in the right direction. But this would only solve the demand side of the inflation problem. To tackle the supply side of the problem the Chinese government would need to use deflationary supply side policies, preferably market-oriented ones. Reducing trade union power would lower the costs to the firms since the workers would have less power "in their efforts to get higher wages." Reducing corporation tax and minimum wage would have the same effect.

Increasing interest would be the most effective solution to slow down economic activity in China, but this must be done in combination with deflationary supply side policies. The government should monitor the unemployment and inflation rate to make sure there is no excessive negative effect on the economy.

16. 'China's Protectionism'

As the argument over China's cheap imports continues, Obama has decided to introduce a protectionist trade policy on the import of tires from China. The goal of this tariff is to decrease the quantity of tires imported which "unfairly undermine American workers." This inflow of cheap tires has already cost the U.S tire industry 5,000 jobs, and as the Chinese tire market continues to expand, and the U.S tire industry continues to lose ground, the United Steelworkers Union decided to file a trade complaint.

The reason behind "the ailing U.S tire industry" is that the U.S and China are currently in a free trade situation. This means that they can trade between each other without artificial barriers and they share a common supply curve. If one country is more efficient at producing a certain good, then it makes sense that it specializes in the production of this good. As China is more efficient in the production of tires, then it will gain a larger share of the world market . This concept is proven by the statement that "over the past five years the volume of Chinese tires in the market has tripled." The downside of this is that China's gain in market share, will draw market share from other countries, and in this case that country is the United States.

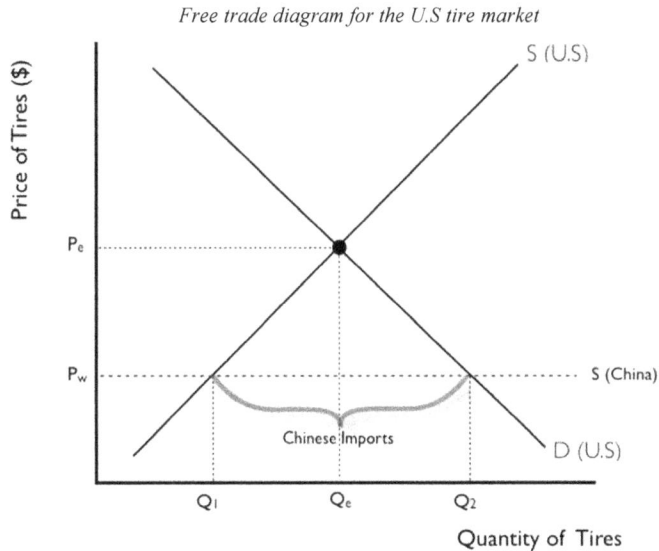

Free trade diagram for the U.S tire market

To protect its market the U.S has opted to impose a tariff, which is a tax charged on imported goods. It argues that it's domestic firms cannot compete with China's cheap tires, and this is causing high levels of structural unemployment as firms are forced to cut production or shut down completely. The tariff will increase the costs to Chinese tire companies "by 35 percent the first year" and this will lead to an increase in U.S domestic production and decreasing unemployment.

From the diagram below we can conclude that the introduction of the tariff will shift Chinese supply upwards and the price of tires will increase. U.S demand for tires will increase from Q_2 to Q_4 as less people will be willing to pay for new tires. Domestic supply on the other hand will increase from Q_3 to Q_1 as the domestic firms will have become more competitive compared to the Chinese suppliers, meaning the U.S government has successfully protected its industries.

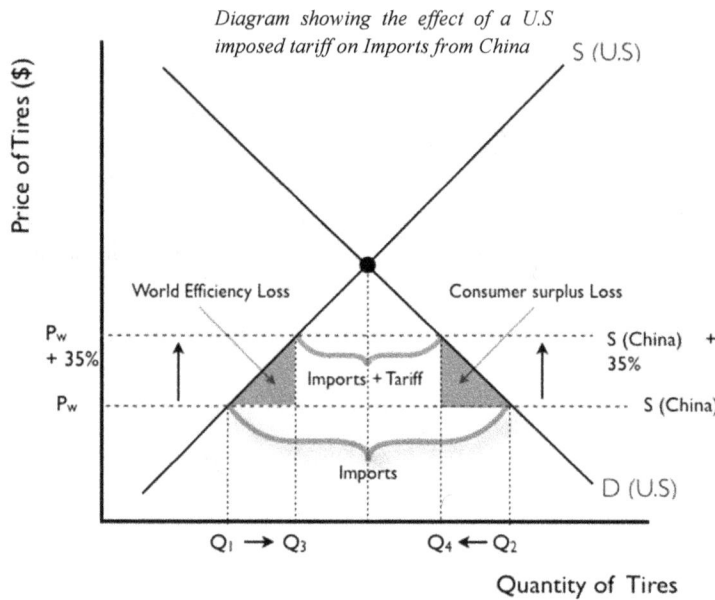

However the U.S government must also consider the consequences. First of all, if the tire industry in America is a sunset industry, meaning it is in decline due to its inability to compete with foreign competition, then the introduction of a tariff may only be temporarily delaying the inevitable. It might be more beneficial to let the industry decline and allocate the freed resources to other sunrise industries.

Secondly the article mentions that this decision "risks angering the nation's second-largest trading partner." It warns that China could feel unfairly disadvantaged by the tariff and might retaliate. China might decide to impose tariffs on some goods it buys from the U.S such as agricultural products. The government will then have temporarily halted the decline of one industry (tires), but it will also have endangered another industry (agriculture) which will suffer as it becomes less competitive due to the Chinese tariff. If this happens then the U.S will be back to square one, or worse.

There is also a deadweight welfare loss which is represented by the red triangle on the right of the tariff diagram. The quantity of tires Q_2 to Q_4 is no longer purchased and they now keep the money they would have otherwise spent. Also, the domestic firms have higher average costs than the Chinese firms and are therefore employing more resources to produce an identical good. These resources are essentially being wasted and this is known as a loss of world efficiency, represented by the triangle on the left.

In conclusion the tariff will temporarily solve the decline of the tire market in the U.S, solving the structural unemployment and benefiting the domestic producers. The drawbacks outweigh this benefit because consumers will be forced to pay a higher price for the same good, Chinese firms will suffer from higher production costs and the risk of retaliation from China is high.

17. 'Venezuela's Strike Boosts Oil Prices' [Re-printed from IBO Economics Guide]

Price elasticity of supply (PES) is the responsiveness of quantity supplied to the changes in the price given. Two major factors that affect the PES of a good are time and availability of producer substitutes. Time influences PES of a good, as the shorter the time period, the more firms are faced with difficulties in controlling the production of the good. For example, assuming surfing suddenly becomes "in thing" which implies demand for surfboards would relatively rise, the shorter the time period the harder the firms will find to expand the production of surfboards. As a result the quantity supplied becomes insensitive to a price change, which is to say the PES of surfboards is inelastic. In the longer term, new firms come into the market, and the existing firms manage to expand production to an adequate level, which consequently makes the PES of surfboards elastic. Availability of producer substitutes (goods that a producer can easily produce as alternatives) also affects the PES of a good. If a product has many substitutes then producers can quickly and easily alter the pattern of production regarding to the price changes. The theory also applies for when a product has fewer or no substitute available. If a good has no producer substitute, the producer has to carry on producing at the same price or withdraws from the market when a price changes, since he would find it difficult to respond flexibly to the variation of prices. In this case, PES of such a good is very inelastic.

The price elasticities of both demand and supply of oil, in this case, tend to be very inelastic. Firstly, there isn't any consumer/producer substitute available for the production of oil. Producers and consumers would find it hard to switch to any alternative, due to the large use of oil in many different industries. Furthermore, the price affecting factors such as the snowstorms and the strike are influencing the oil industry in the short run, which contributes to the PES of the oil being inelastic. The US demands heating fuels instantly after the snowstorms regardless of its price, as it is a necessity during the cold weather. Necessities are generally bought at whatever price, as they tend to have very inelastic price elasticity of demand. Therefore an immediate increase in the oil price would barely reduce the quantity demanded, due to its low elasticity.

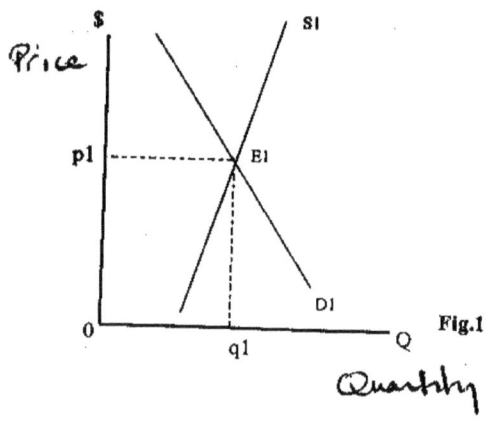

Fig.1

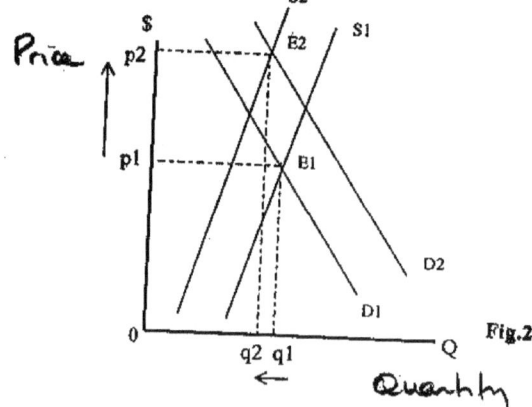

Fig.2

The price rise is mainly because of disturbance by the strike in refining and shipping operation, and of snowstorms in the United States. As seen in Fig.2, the strike has shifted the supply curve to the left reducing the general supply level, because of disruption to the oil suppliers. The snowstorms in the US contributed to a sharp increase in the demand for heating fuel, which lead the demand curve to shift to its right.

As a result of these changes, the equilibrium price has gone up from p1 to p2, and the quantity supplied has decreased from q1 to q2; meaning that less of the product is being bought at a higher price. However, these on-going changes are only in the short run, therefore after a certain period of time, for example in this case, after the impact of the snowstorms fade away and the strike is over, the curves will eventually find a new equilibrium.

At the moment, because of the present political situation, the market is very cautious. The oil prices could fluctuate at anytime. If the US should declare war on Iraq, there would be procurement demand for oil, which could boost up the price of oil extremely higher than its usual level because more oil is being demanded and the PES of oil is very inelastic due to the short time period. The current situation, where Venezuela might increase its crude oil output and the cartel is continuing to supply above the official production limit whilst the demand for the oil escalates, could depreciate the price of oil, and such overproduction is alarming as it could also lead to depletion of the resource itself.

18. 'Top Japanese council 'plans tax cuts of $4b' [Re-printed from IBO Economics Guide]

Japan's 'top economic council is planning tax cuts worth 200 to 300 billion yen, to help pull the economy out of an 18-month long recession[i].' This is known as Fiscal Policy, and it could 'promote investment' and encourage 'purchases of homes,' as it would give the Japanese consumer more disposable income, perhaps increasing aggregate demand[ii].

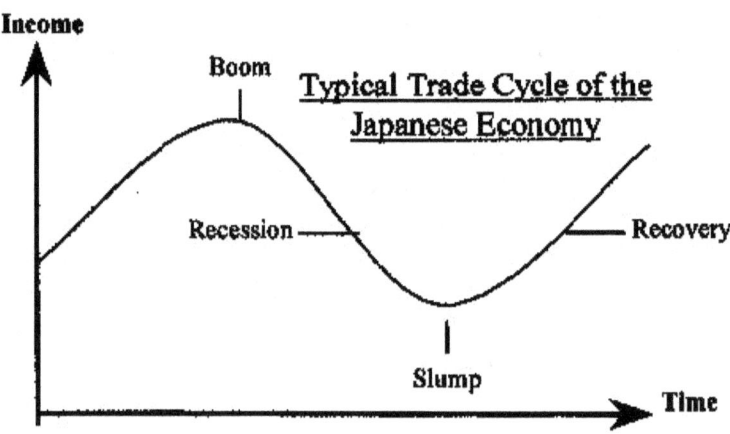

Extra investment would be an injection into the circular flow. If firms manage 'to boost their international competitiveness,' through 'investment related to research and development,' Japanese exports could increase, which would mean another injection into the circular flow. These injections, coupled by a decrease in taxation (a form of withdrawal), could lead to economic growth as the economy expands due to the multiplier effect.[iii]

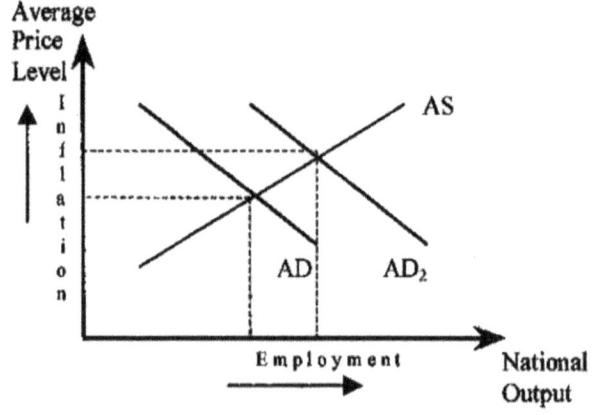

On the aggregate demand and supply diagram, the vertical axis actually measures inflation and the horizontal axis is a measure of national output. If the aggregate demand curve were to shift AD→AD$_2$ right, output (and employment) would increase.

Lower taxes would encourage saving, which provides a source of financial capital for firms to borrow from. The council specifically mentions cutting taxes 'on corporate capital spending' to 'ease the burden on firms that spend money on investment and research.' Also, by lowering 'corporate taxes,' firms could be prompted to produce more, as they would be getting a bigger share of the revenue generated by receipts.

This policy, however, has several potential weaknesses. In theory it is an 'inflationary policy;' there is an inherent 'trade-off' between growth and inflation. However, Japan is currently facing deflation, and with interest rates hovering at around 0% inflation is definitely not a concern. Japan's dull economic climate, though, could truncate the effectiveness of such a policy, because the marginal propensity to consume[iv] would be fairly low, given the high unemployment and poor confidence (or 'animal spirits') in the economy. Instead, extra income is likely to be saved rather than invested, and thus the multiplier effect could be insufficient. According to Keynesian theory, the Balanced Budget Multiplier could perhaps be more effective. If the government were to tax the citizens and then inject the tax back into the circular flow (by increasing government expenditure), the multiplier effect would be larger by the initial amount of the tax. If the majority of the tax were paid through savings (and the Japanese are saving a lot), then national income could increase by a greater amount. However, such actions could further tighten the wallets of a weary and frugal people.

Tax relief could also bring about supply-side incentives: lowering corporate taxes could encourage increased production. Additionally, 'research and development' could bring about improved productivity, as they would make production more efficient, and this in turn could lead to an increase in aggregate supply[v.]

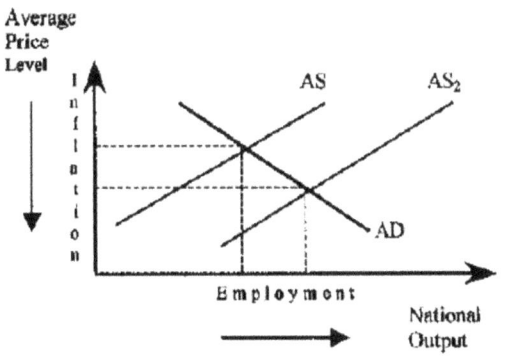

The proposed tax cuts could push aggregate supply out (AS→AS₂) increasing national income and perhaps helping Japan out of recession.

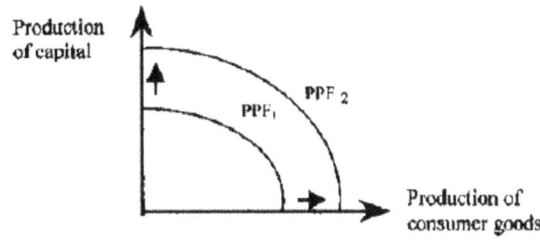

Additionally, investment on capital will increase Japan's productive capacity, expanding the production possibility frontier, and shifting the long-run Aggregate Supply curve out.

However, lowering 'corporate taxes' may not be as beneficial as the council hopes. Firms could simply pass on higher profits to their shareholders, instead of using the extra funds for investment. The policy could even backfire, with firms reducing production and maintaining their current level of profits (profit-satisficing). Consider the Laffer Curve below.

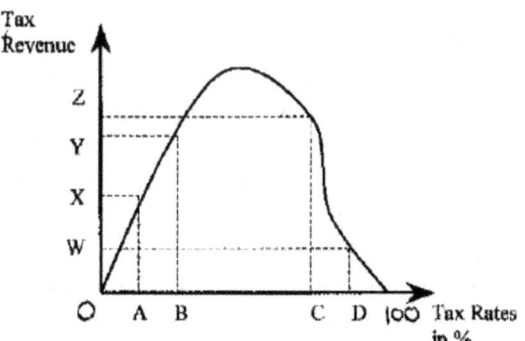

At a tax rate of D, a decrease in taxes to C will cause revenue to go up from W to Z as there is greater incentive to produce. If the tax rate is at C however, a decrease in taxes to B will bring about a fall in revenue from Z to Y, as firms may choose instead to grant workers more leisure time and keep unions happy or 'profit-satisfice'.

The tax relief plan could also lead to increased inequality. There will be less tax to redistribute income, while the richer classes, who tend to own the majority of resources in the industry, will benefit from lower corporate taxes as their profits increase. Also, the government will lose tax revenue, and this may hinder its ability to provide education, healthcare etc. for the poor.

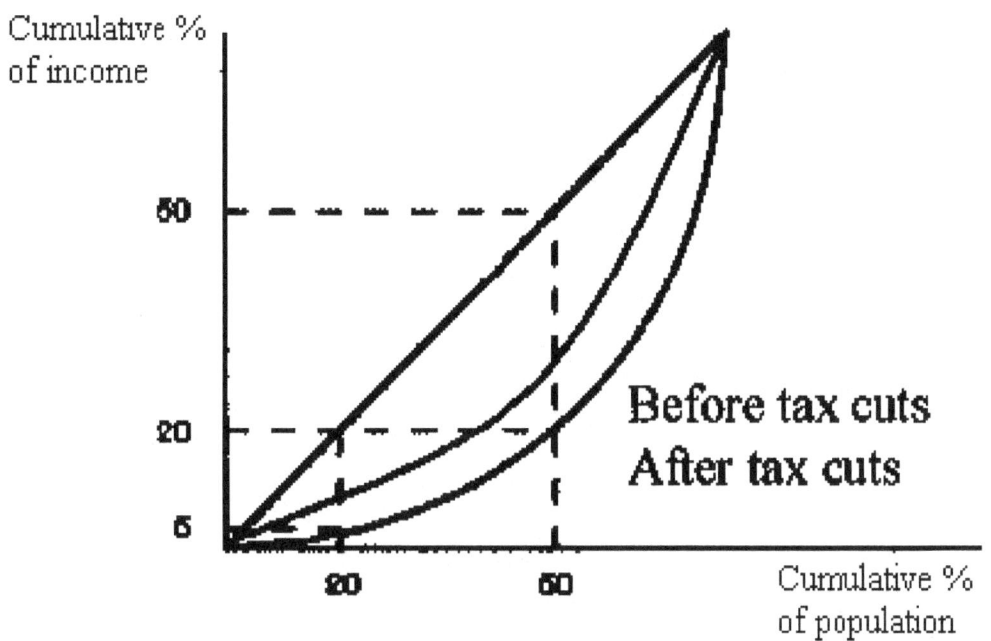

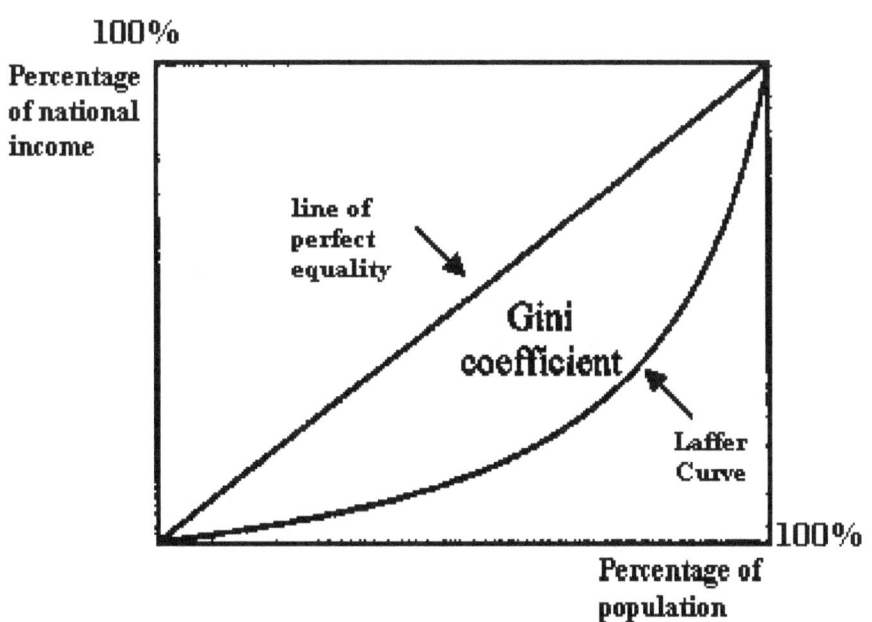

As the distribution of income becomes more unequal, the value of the Gini coefficient increases. In the most unequal distribution, the Gini value is 1.

In conclusion, the proposed tax relief plan could be an effective method to help Japan recover from the recession. Detailed analysis, however, highlights several potential weaknesses of the policy, as it may not be enough to revitalize Japan's economy. It may even backfire, prompting consumers to save more or work less, as illustrated by the Laffer Curve. The tax cuts are not as favourable to the poor classes, who they tend to own disproportionately less of the factors of production (Land, Labour, Capital, Skilled Management). Tax cuts would likely increase income inequality, and a loss in tax revenue would force the government to decrease spending in other areas. Japanese P.M Junichiro Koizumi is having a tumultuous time in office, and perhaps these tax cuts are a form of 'politicisation' to the elite classes, who have more political influence. In the end, though, tax relief will not be enough; Japan needs to bring about the 'revitalisation of domestic industries, structural reforms and the tackling of bad loans,' as the council acknowledges.

[i] Recession can be defined as two consecutive quarters of negative growth.
[ii] Aggregate Demand is the total expenditure of goods and service on economy in one year. AD = C+I+G+(X-M), where C = consumer expenditure, I= investment expenditure, G = government expenditure and (X-M) = net exports (exports-imports)
[iii] The 'multiplier' is a function in the circular flow of income, which serves to multiply the effect of any injections or withdrawals according to the level of the mpc (see below).
[iv] The MPC measure the proportion of additional income that is spent on households.
[v] Aggregate Supply can be defined as the total level of output in the whole economy at any given level of average prices.

19. 'Markets Fall Out of Love With Cinderella Currency' [Re-printed from IBO Economics Guide]

Until recently, "robust economic growth, attractive interest rates and a healthy fiscal position" strengthened Britain's currency, the Sterling pound. However, "since the start of the year", the pound has depreciated[1], against other currencies such as the Euro. The reasons for this are the expected reduction in interest rates by the Bank of England, the depreciation of the American dollar, the increase in Britain's current account deficit and the political instability caused by the uncertainty from the conflict with Iraq.

A reduction in interest rates from 4% "to 3.25 per cent" is expected as consumer demand, a component of the total demand in the economy, weakens due to a rise in saving and expected increases in taxes. While the use of monetary policy may revive waning consumer demand, it may also lead to the pound's depreciation. This is because British residents and foreigners may choose to deposit their money in countries like Australia with relatively higher interest rates as they will earn a higher return on their savings there. This will increase the supply of the pound in international foreign exchange markets from S to Sl while decreasing demand for the pound from D to Dl (See diagram 1). The price of the pound in Australian dollars and other currencies would fall from PI to P2, leading to its depreciation.

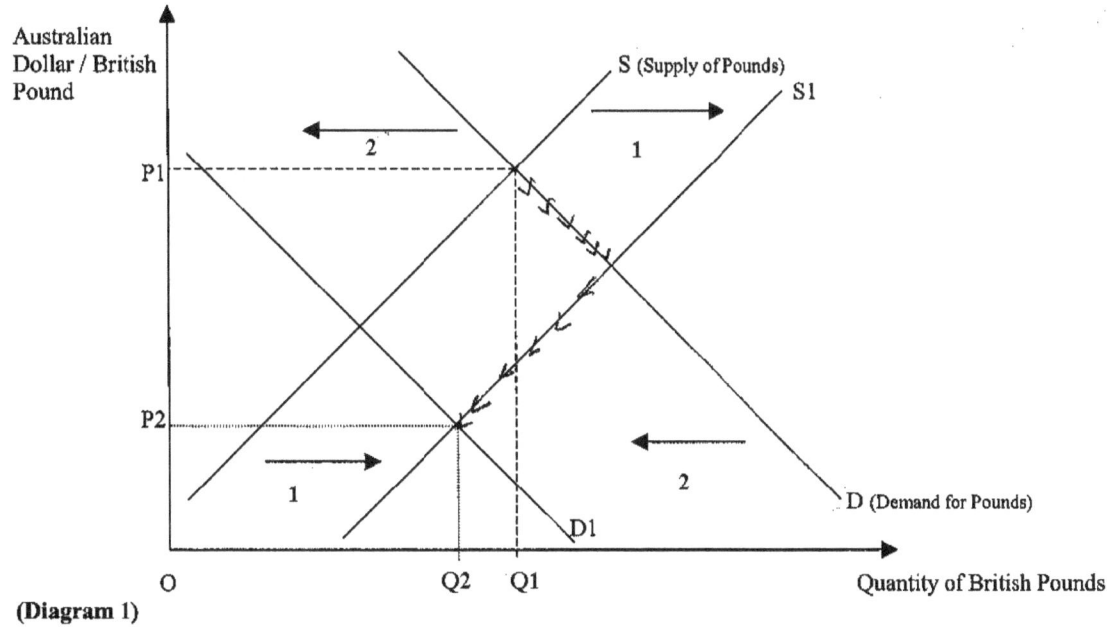

(Diagram 1)

Secondly, "economic problems confronting" America have depreciated the American Dollar, making British exports to American markets more expensive. Thus, a fall in demand for British exports would decrease quantity demand for the British pound from Ql to Q2 and the price of the pound in American dollars falls from PI to P2 (See diagram 2 in next page).

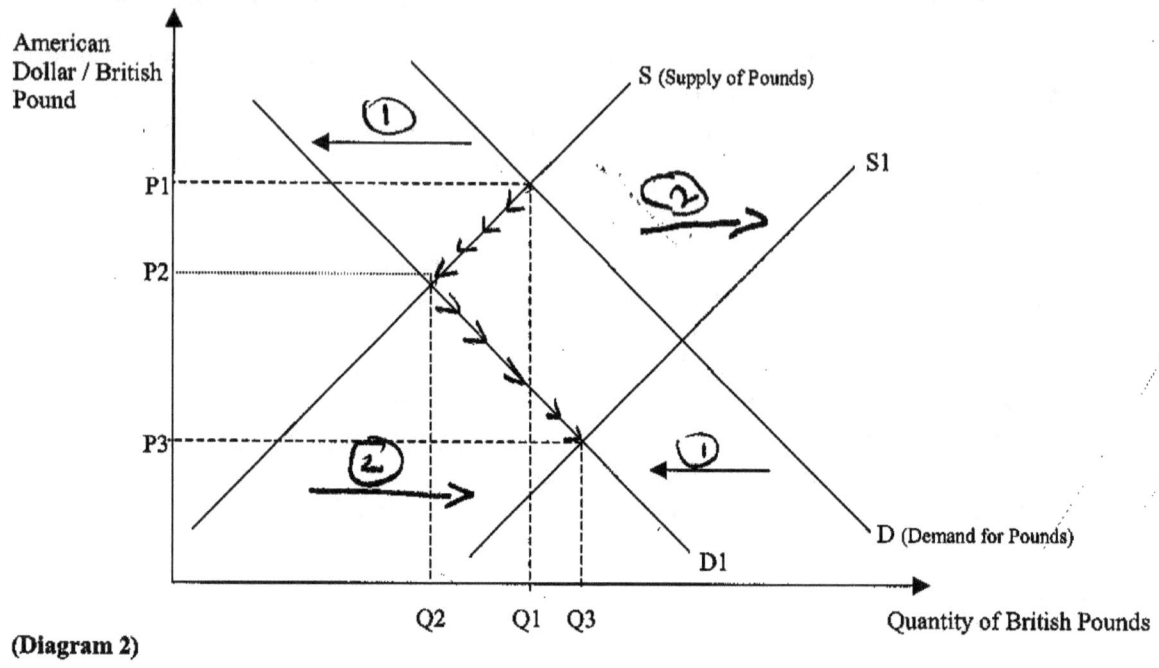

(Diagram 2)

Britain's ballooning current account deficit[2] may have also contributed to the depreciation of the pound. A probable increase in consumer expenditure on imports would have likely created and expanded the current account deficit. Thus, the supply of the pound in international foreign exchange markets will rise as the pound is exchanged for the currencies of the countries that Britain secures its imports from. Hence, an increase in the supply of the pound from Q1 to Q3 (See diagram 2), would lead to its depreciation against other currencies. In this case, the price of the pound in American dollars falls from P1 to P3 (See diagram 2).

Finally, the uncertain political future of the ruling Conservative Party due to the possible conflict with Iraq has reduced the confidence that investors and speculators have on the British economy. Hence, speculators may choose to sell the pound thereby increasing its supply, while buyers may wait for the pound to fall, reducing demand for it and leading to its depreciation.

A positive ramification that could accompany the depreciation of the pound is the reduction in Britain's current account deficit. A weaker pound would increase the price of imports and reduce demand for them. Furthermore, British exports, which would tend to have a high price elasticity of demand[3], will become more competitive. Thus an increase in demand of British exports from Q1 to Q2 would increase the total revenue Britain earns from its exports from P1 to P2 (See diagram 3). Hence, a fall in Britain's debits and an increase in its credits would improve the country's current account balance, a macro-economic objective.

Secondly, the expected reduction in interest rates and a rise in the prices of imports may boost consumer demand for domestic goods and services. This could increase domestic employment and avert a recession[4].

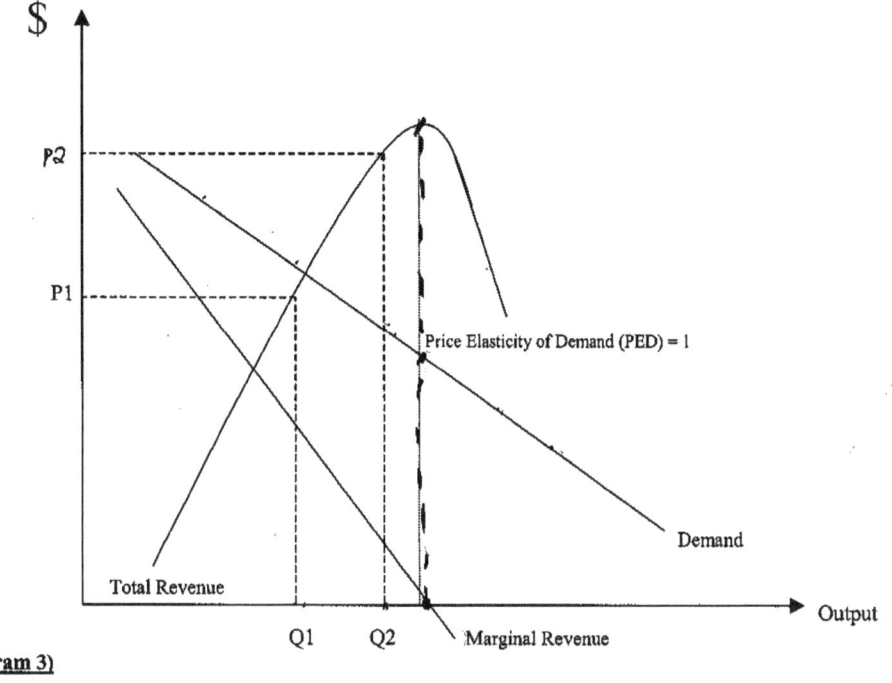

(Diagram 3)

However, Britain's economic prospects are likely to "look distinctly less rosy", in the short-term. "Chill winds blowing through the international economy" may not significantly increase demand for British exports while import expenditure would rise as importers take time to realise the change in import prices. Subsequently, the British economy is likely to experience a greater current account deficit before its current account balance improves.

Furthermore, the lack of confidence in the pound and a reduction in interest rates may channel away long-term capital investment and short-term deposits to other countries such as New-Zealand. This may lead to a deficit in Britain's capital account[5] and make funding a large current account deficit more difficult. Therefore, while the depreciation of the pound is expected to hurt the British economy, such difficulties may only persist in the short-term and economic prospects for Britain are likely to improve with the depreciation of the pound.

[1] A fall in the free market exchange rate of the pound against foreign currencies.
[2] The current account records imports and exports of goods and services, interest, profits and dividends flowing into or out of the country and transfers of money like grants.
[3] The Price elasticity of demand measures the responsiveness of demand due to a change in price.
[4] A recession is 2 quarters of negative economic growth.
[5] Records investment and other financial flows into and out of the country.

20. 'Oxfam Takes on The Coffee Kings' [Re-printed from IBO Economics Guide]

A critical aspect of development economics is the terms of trade. Individual countries earn foreign currency from selling their exports abroad and spend this money on imports. For instance, if a country like Burundi exports coffee and imports machinery, and a supply-side shock like unusually good harvesting conditions causes a massive increase in the coffee supply and thus a fall in coffee prices (Diagram One), Burundi must export more coffee (which, due to the labour-intensity of farming methods could lead to a decrease in unemployment) in order to finance its imports. Burundi's terms of trade have thus become more adverse.

Diagram One: Decrease in Coffee Prices due to Increased Supply

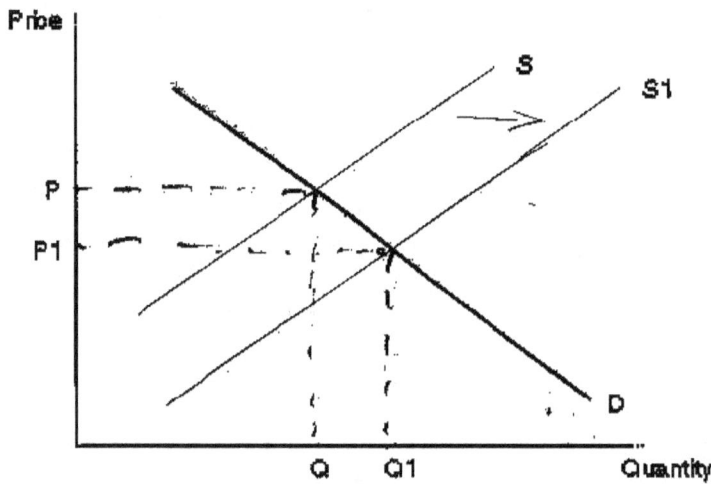

The key element is not the monetary price of coffee but its price compared to other goods. Burundi may find itself in a detrimental position not only because the processing of coffee (which adds to its value) is done outside Burundi, but also because the world price of commodities has gradually tended to fall relative to the price of manufactures like machinery or other capital goods.

This trend may actually encourage Burundi - and many other developing nations that largely export primary products and import manufactures - to export more coffee beans (to maintain their export revenue) while there are shortages of coffee at home. This same situation occurs in southern Somalia where bananas are exported to foreign markets yet there is widespread starvation at home. Moreover, there is often a high Gini coefficient (Diagram Two) in these countries and a rich elite is determining that 'essential' imports include luxury items like televisions or automobiles. Therefore, as the standards of living are declining so too are the terms of trade worsening and, for the majority, poverty increases.

Diagram Two: Lorenz Curve and High Gini Coefficient Reflecting Income Inequality

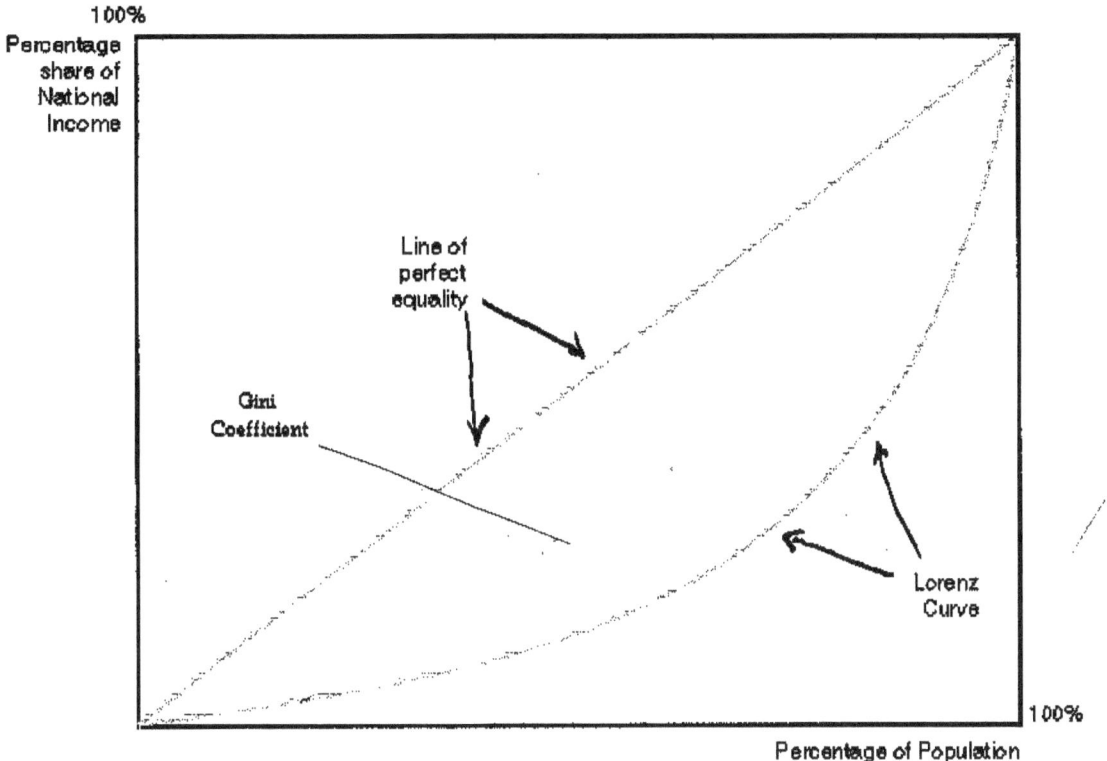

Yet, importantly, it is not only trade of visibles that counts when investigating development. Due to the debt crisis, a significant proportion[1] of the revenue generated from coffee exports is repaid to Western banks so, as more goods are exported, the wealth of several debt-laden African nations does not improve and people continue starving, while Western nations gain.

This is the dire situation that grips African nations yet some growth and development strategies offer hope for improvement. Yet while the author criticises IMF policies like export-led growth, which is removing trade barriers and building growth through trade and has been followed by Singapore and other Asian Tiger economies, there are several distinct advantages of adopting such a policy. The ambiguous concept of 'fairness' is frequently mentioned in this article, and a policy such as export-led growth is arguably economically 'fair' as it encourages countries to make the most of their factor endowments and follow comparative advantage, developing industries in which they can produce goods with a lower opportunity cost than other countries. Furthermore it could lead many African countries (as has happened with Taiwan) away from producing primary products to producing manufactured goods and thus, by the W Arthur Lewis Structural Change Model, could lead to increased economic development. However, it can lead to a degree of exploitation as developed countries could drain resources and, more recently, the days of developing through export-led growth are dwindling due to the trend of increased protectionism (for instance, the massive EU and US subsidies to farmers).

Furthermore, and this is particularly true of decolonised countries like Kenya and South Africa, the benefits from export-led trading may not accrue to the Kenyan and South African nationals as profits are repatriated by European or American landowners.

For real and long-term development to occur, there must be a degree of international cooperation between the wealthier importers like the EU and poorer coffee producers like Tanzania. Since Tanzanian farmers cannot afford to decently educate children or provide adequate healthcare, their production possibility frontier cannot develop significantly but if more money were invested into education and health, improving the quality and quantity of labour, then the PFF could shift outwards and economic development would occur. While Tanzania has tried to shift the terms of trade in its favour by not only growing and harvesting the coffee crop (and so collecting only about 1% of coffee revenues) but also trying to roast, ship and package instant coffee themselves (which would, it is estimated, bring in 45% of the coffee revenues), they have only been knocked back by European protectionism and massive tariffs which ensure that lower-priced (but inefficient and higher-cost) European producers sell more coffee. This example of trade diversion is not uncommon, and illustrates some of the many problems developing countries that export commodities, like coffee, face.

[1] Africa spends four times more on debt repayment than healthcare.

21. 'Gasoline Tax in West Virginia'

The article highlights West Virginia's plan to gain revenue from the higher tax on gasoline which is price inelastic in demand and should increase consumers' expenditures.

Price elasticity of demand (PED) is a measure of the responsiveness of the quantity demanded for a good with respect to a change in the price of the good. The major factors of PED are availability of substances, time span involved and the proportion of income spent on the good. When PED < 1 then a good/service is price inelastic.

Gasoline has an inelastic demand. There are few substitutes of gasoline in short run. It means that the quantity of gasoline demanded does not decrease much when the price increases. See Figure 1.

Figure 1: West Virginia: Gasoline is price inelastic in demand

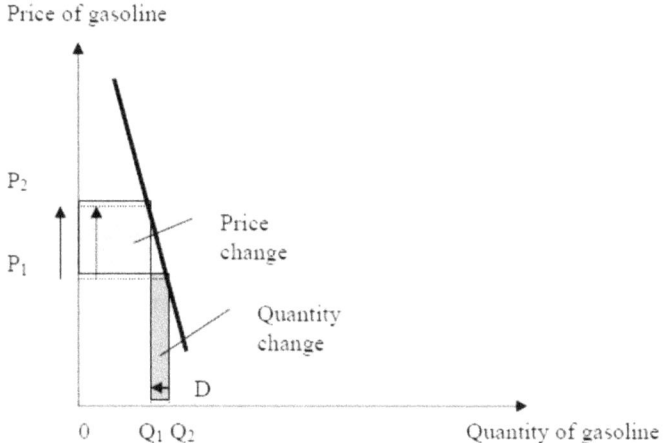

Price of gasoline increased from P1 to P2 and quantity demanded should reduce from 0Q1 to 0Q2. Price fluctuation (yellow area) is large in comparison with expected quantity decrease (green area). It means although sellers increase price consumers reduce their purchase very little.

Complementary goods/services are those which need one another. Revenue is a full amount of the tax. Gasoline and vehicles are complementary goods. The increase of gasoline price should influence market of cars. Consumers who see gasoline price increases will not buy large cars. See Figure 2.

Figure 2: West Virginia: Price change of gasoline influence on cars' market.

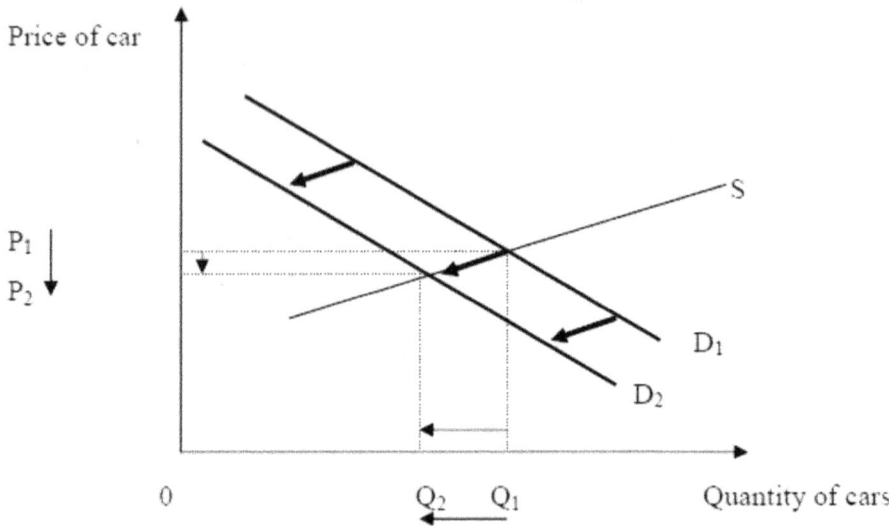

Change in gasoline market would decrease large car market. The prices would decrease from P1 to P2. It should not be a big price change however the demand curve would shift from D1 to D2.

Total revenue is the total income of the firm. Sellers should reduce supply of gasoline because of higher price. It is profitable to decrease supply of inelastic gasoline. See Figure 3.

Figure 3: West Virginia: Total revenue rises

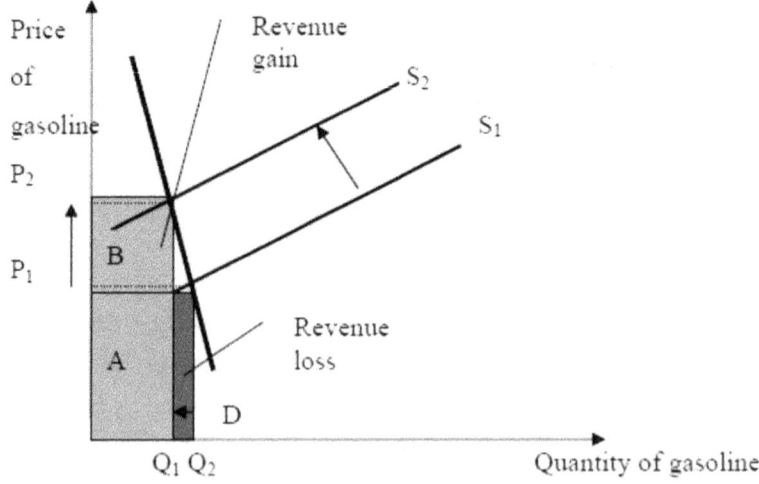

Supply is reduced from S1 to S2. However it causes a bigger revenue gain (blue area) than a revenue loss (green area). Total revenue, A and B, increases.

A specific or flat rate tax is a specific amount of money put on a good/service. Incidence of tax shows how much pay the buyer or the seller or both. Government increased flat rate tax 4.5 cents per–gallon. In the short run the tax could be an effective source of revenue. See Figure 4.

Figure 4: West Virginia: Flat rate tax

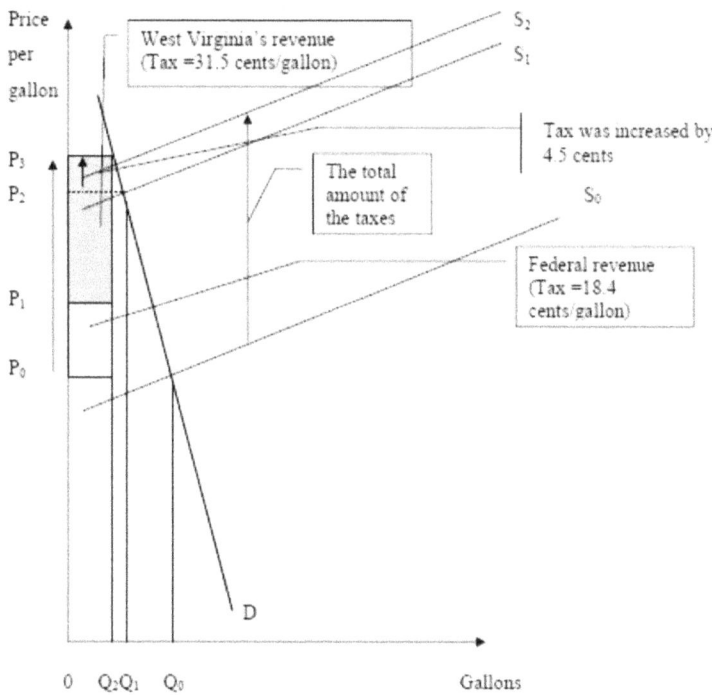

Difference between P2 and P3 is 4.5 cents/per-gallon and it is an additional sum to state tax of gasoline. Government revenue is equal to 31.5 x 0Q2. Earlier government gain was equal to 27 x 0Q1. Government is expected to get higher revenue. Although, the price from P0 to P3 seems to be the same as the full amount of the taxes but truly it is not. See Figure 5.

Figure 5: West Virginia: The full amount of taxes and buyer expenditures per-gallon

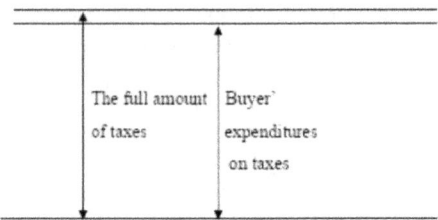

Price increases less than total amount of the taxes. Buyer' expenditures reflect amount of money which consumers pay of the full amount of taxes. The remaining small part of the full amount of taxes curve is seller' expenditures. See Figure 6.

Figure 6: West Virginia: Incidence of taxes

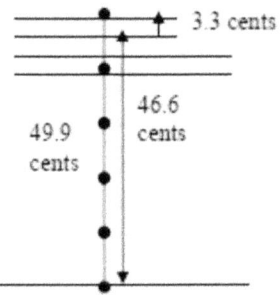

Buyers pay almost the full amount of taxes; about 46.6 cents per gallon compared to only 3.3 cents per gallon by sellers. It should cause a loss of satisfaction to consumers. Consumers have two choices. They can buy gasoline at higher price in West Virginia or they can buy it in nearest states where taxes are lower. The second choice will not impact consumers by taxes, but then retailers could not sell gasoline and gain profit and instead of this they "will have to pay the tax on the gas they already have in stock as of January 1". (1) The amount of gas which is in stock is limited and then retailers will pay all taxes for government West Virginia will not maximize total revenue. It is very possible that all consumers will leave West Virginia to fill their tanks with cheaper gasoline; however if most consumers buy gasoline in other states retailers and later government will not gain. PED of gasoline in long run term is more elastic. Gasoline has substitutes such as diesel, gas, electricity, but they are not very close to gasoline. However, in long run term people can start using substitutes of gasoline.

In the conclusion, government expectations are not very calculated. Instead of gaining more, West Virginia can damage local market of gasoline. People instead of paying high taxes can easily buy gasoline in states where it is not so expensive. In long run term PED for gasoline can become more price elastic because people can use substitutes. Therefore, West Virginia should find other solutions to gain bigger revenues because an increase in petrol excise could substantially damage its economy.

22. 'Fed lowers outlook for growth in 2008'

This article highlights the US Central Bank's use of monetary policy through interest rates to influence economic growth. Specifically to avoid stagflation. Stagflation occurs when the economy experiences a decline in economic growth plus rising inflation.

Unemployment rate is the number of unemployed expressed as a percentage of the total labour force. US unemployment in October was 4.7%. The Federal Reserve expects that next year it should rise to 4.8-4.9%.1 Such a change would still lead to economy with full employment rate. See Figure 1.

Figure 1: US: Full Employment Equilibrium

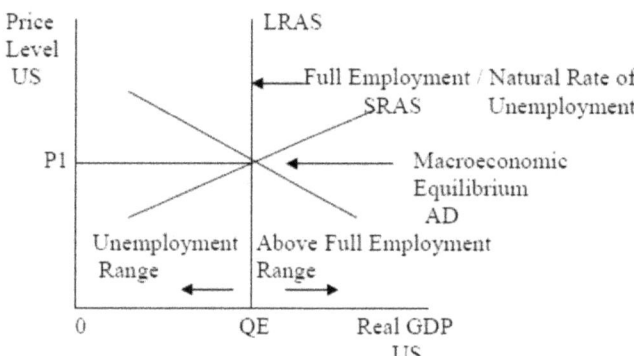

The US economy is operating at full capacity where SRAS = AD = LRAS, Real GDP is maximized and the Price level is at P1. However, unemployment is increasing which leads to decrease in economic growth.

Economic growth is an increase in a country's Real GDP per capita. US economic growth for 2008 is expected to be at 1.8% while in 2007 it is 2.5%.2 See Figure 2.

Figure 2: US Potential decrease in Economic growth

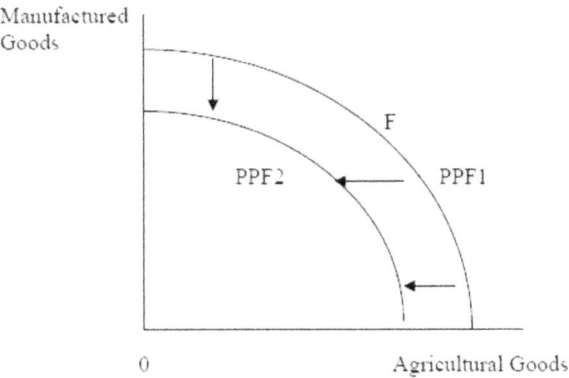

When the PPF shifts to the left, from PPF1 to PPF2, potential output decreases.

Aggregate demand is the relationship between the aggregate quantity of goods and services demanded-or Real GDP- and the price level. AD =C+I+G+X-M. US economy is influenced by the surge in energy prices, decrease in housing growth and lower level of job growth. It could cause weaker consumer spending which would reduce AD. See Figure 3.

Figure 3: US Decrease in Aggregate Demand

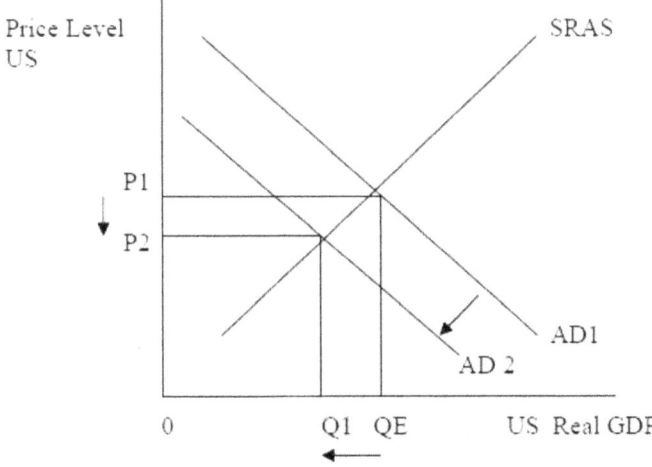

The AD curve shifts to the left from AD1 to AD2. The price level decreases from P1 to P2, good for price stability. New external equilibrium is where SRAS=AD2. Real GDP decreases from 0QE to 0Q1. The reduce in GDP will result in an increase in unemployment. The decline in Real GDP will worsen the macroeconomic objectives of Economic Growth, Economic Development and Full Employment.

The risk of stagflation is very high due to cost-push inflation. In 2008 the US economy along with the rest of the world, is facing increasing oil and food prices. For example, oil prices are surging to US$100/barrel. The SRAS will shift to the left. See Figure 4.

Figure 4: US Cost-Push Inflation

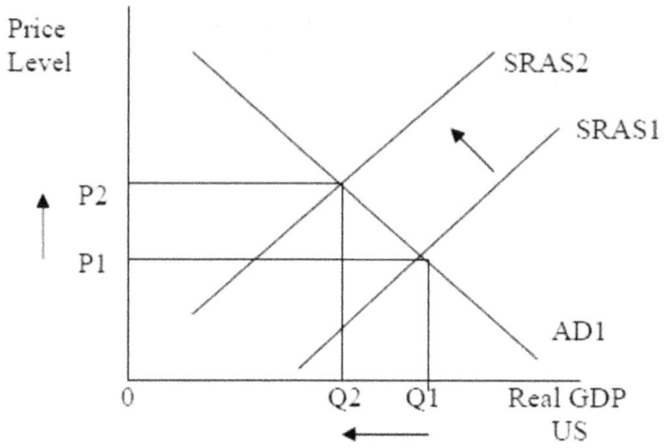

The SRAS Curve shifts from SRAS1 to SRAS2. Real GDP decreases from 0Q1 to 0Q2. The Price Level increases from P1 to P2.

So, the main problems in US are increased unemployment and inflation-stagflation. In order to solve these problems monetary or/and fiscal policies could be adopted.

Stagflation becomes a dilemma for monetary policy when policies usually used to increase economic growth will further increase inflation while policies used to reduce inflation will further the decline of an already-declining economy. Monetary policy refers to changes in the money supply and interest rates to affect aggregate demand and aggregate supply. In US, monetary policy is controlled by Federal Reserve. To increase AD, the Fed should increase the money supply which decreases interest rates. See Figure 5.

Figure 5: US: Increase in Money Supply

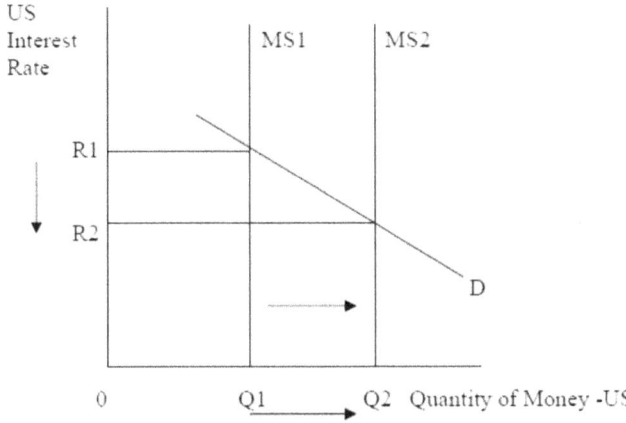

The Fed increase a money supply results in a shift in the money supply curve from MS1 to MS2. Interest rates fall from R1 to R2. The shift made by the Fed decreases borrowing costs to consumers. Besides, it gives an increase in the components C of AD.

By lowering interest rates, the cost for consumers to buy products on credit and businesses to borrow to expand production are reduced. While this can increase economic activity, it can also result in increased inflation.

The monetary mechanism in order to reduce inflation should raise interest rates, which would increase the cost for consumers to buy products on credit and businesses to borrow to expand production. While this could reduce inflation, it could also result in decreased economic activity.

Inflation is a sustained increase in the general price level. The predictions for the 2010 is a decrease of inflation rate in the range of 1.6% to 1.9%3 which is below creeping inflation level. See Figure 4.

Figure 4: US Deflation

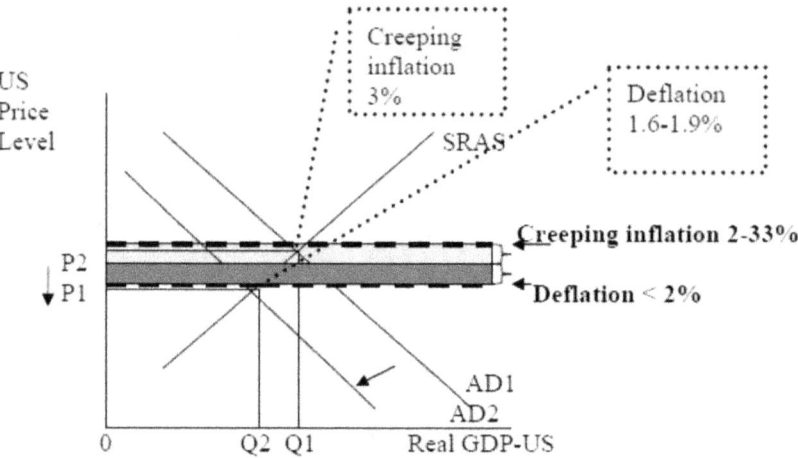

US healthy creeping inflation rate is predicting to change into unhealthy deflation rate. Deflation should have negative impact on producers' profits which would result in less investment by firms. Besides, assets would lose value. Banks would also be less willing to lend in periods of deflation. However, while the Fed is reducing interest rates inflation could not be reduced and achieve deflation.

In conclusion, since US is going into recession in 2008 it needs to use policies which could reduce inflation and decrease unemployment because what happens in US would affect all world economies. A very difficult economic balance.

23. 'US to impose penalty tariffs on China'

This article highlights China's unfair trade with US, a major cause of US rising trade deficit. Anti-dumping could help US to solve this economic problem. Fair trade is a trading partnership which seeks greater equity in international trade. A trade deficit is a negative value of difference between the sum of visible export and the sum of visible import. US has a substantial and growing trade deficit with China. See Table1 and Diagram1.

Table 1: China's Trade with the United States ($ billion)

	1995	1996	1997	1998	1999	2000	2001	2002	2003	2004	2005	2006
US Exports	11.8	12.0	12.8	14.3	13.1	16.3	19.2	22.1	28.4	34.7	41.8	55.2
% change	26.9	1.7	6.7	10.9	-8.0	24.4	18.3	15.1	28.5	22.2	20.6	32.0
US Imports	45.6	51.5	62.6	71.2	81.8	100.0	102.3	125.2	152.4	196.7	243.5	287.8
% change	17.5	13.0	21.5	13.8	14.9	22.3	2.2	22.4	21.7	29.1	23.8	18.2
Total trade	57.4	63.5	75.4	85.5	94.9	116.3	121.5	147.3	180.8	231.4	285.3	343.0
% change	19.3	10.6	18.7	13.4	11.0	22.6	21.4	21.2	22.8	28.0	23.3	20.2
US trade imbalance with China	-33.8	-39.5	-49.8	-56.9	-68.7	-83.7	-83.0	-103.1	-124.0	-162.0	-201.6	-232.5

Diagram 1: Total trade and US trade deficit

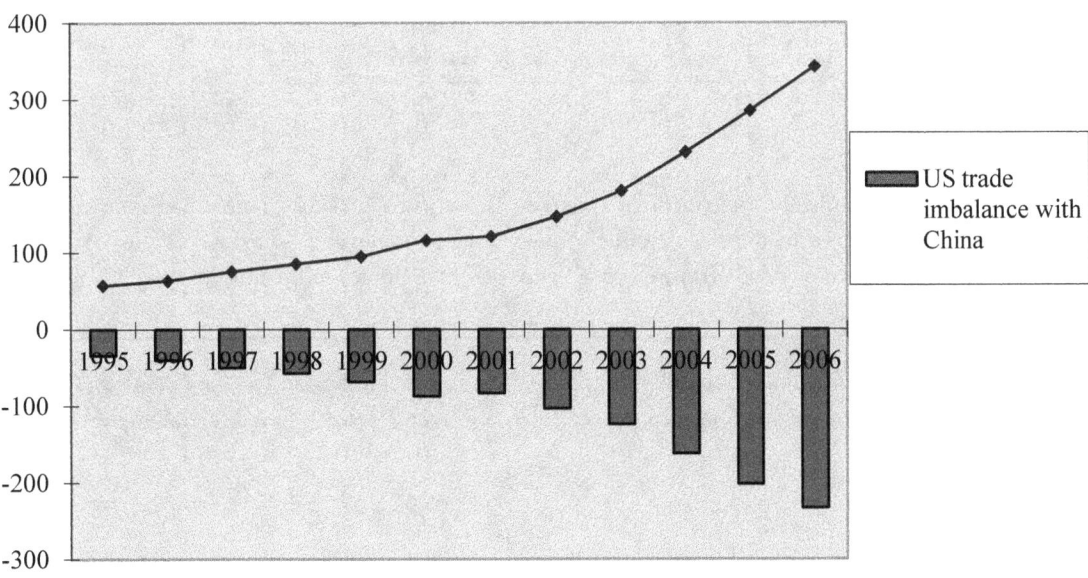

Total merchandise trade between China and US increased to US$ 343 billion in 2006. However, US imports more than exports, causing increasing annual trade deficit from US$ 33.8 billion in 1995 to US$ 232.5 billion in 2006.

A subsidy is a financial grant from government which acts as an incentive to producers to produce more and lower the costs of production. Chinese economic policy is to provide domestic producers with subsidies in order to lower cost of production and increase supply. See Diagram 2.

Diagram2: The effect of the subsidy in China

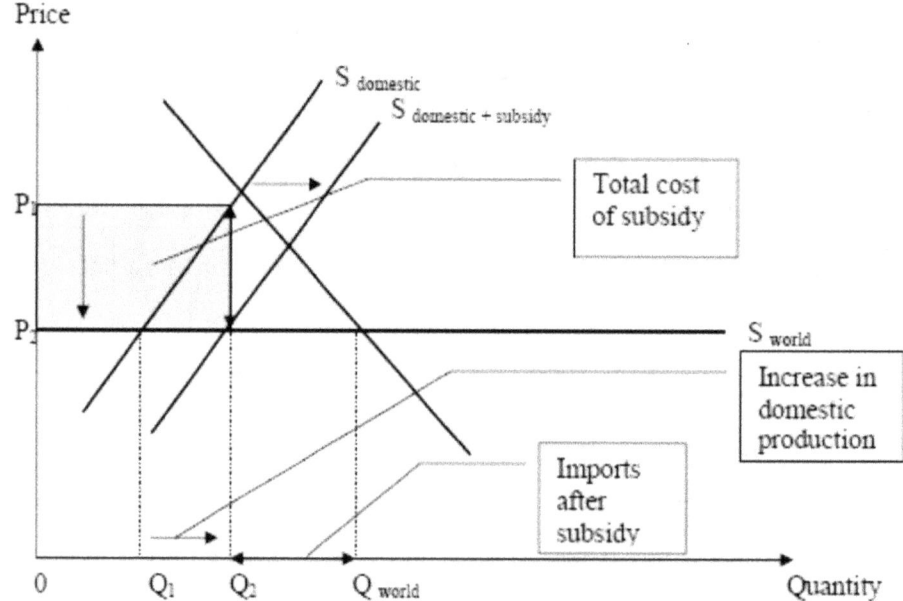

Diagram 2 reflects how a subsidy affects China's market. Because of subsidy China's domestic suppliers are able to shift supply curve to the right from S domestic to S domestic + subsidy. Yellow area is a subsidy, which reduces price of goods from P1 to P2 and increases domestic quantity of goods from 0 Q1 to 0Q2.

Because of lower price and increased quantity of goods China imports less from foreign countries. China's producers are able to sell goods on foreign markets such as US at a price below the US domestic price level. See Diagram 3.

Diagram3: Effect of China's subsidies on exports to US.

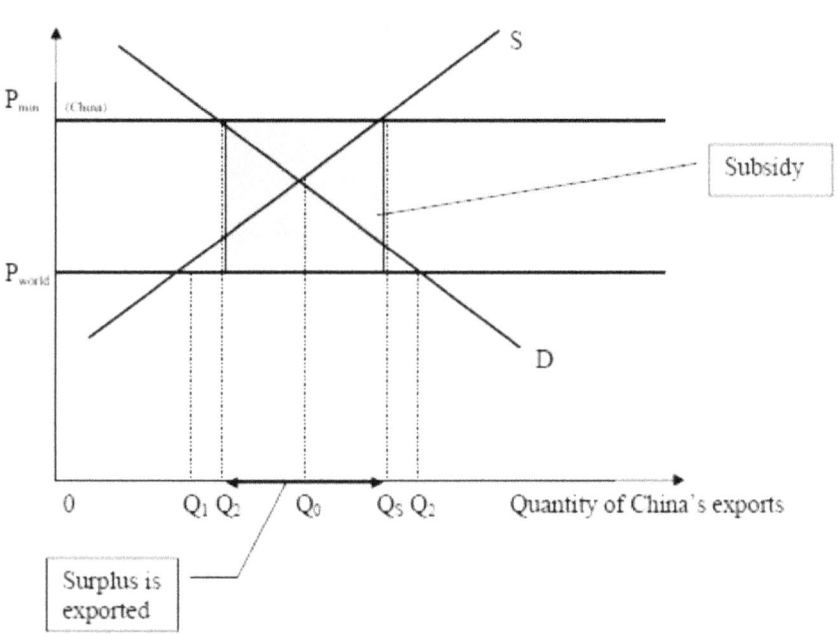

China's producers are able to produce goods at lower prices because of subsidy but US producers are not able to as their costs are higher. An amount from Q2 to QS is China's surplus of production and a part of this production is exported to US at low price.

World Trade Organization (WTO) is an organization which main principles are non-discrimination, stabile trade environment, fair competition, development and free trade through negotiation. US and China are in the WTO, which is focused on anti-dumping and reducing subsidies. China gains an unfair competitive advantage over other members.

The problem can be resolved by anti-dumping or countervailing duties. An anti – dumping tariff is a tax on imported goods in order to reflect "true" cost of production. This tariff will let US producers to compete with China's producers because tariffs on China's production will increase the price of goods. See Diagram 4.

Diagram 4: The effects of a US tariff on China's exports to US

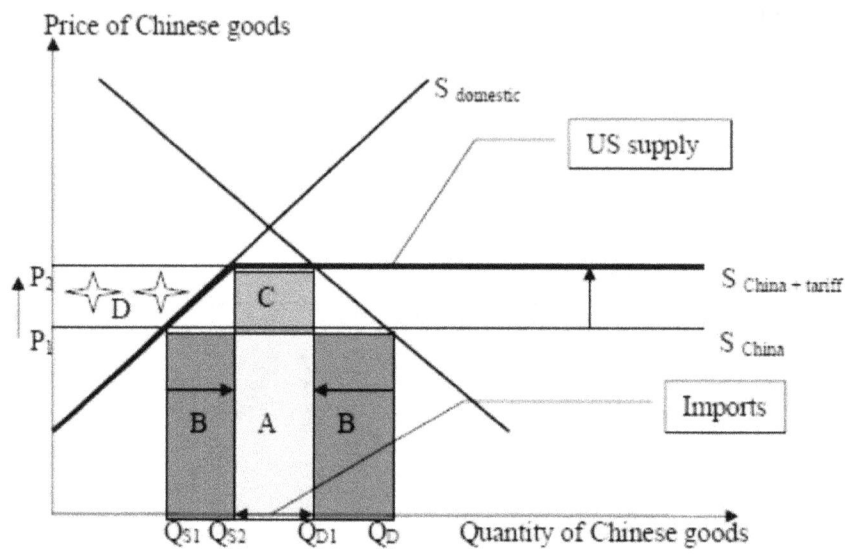

Diagram 4 shows how tariffs could increase China's selling prices. US tariffs will increase prices of Chinese goods from P1 to P2 and decrease China's revenue from the amount BAB to the amount A. An area A is Chinese goods exports to US. An area C is tax revenue to US government and an area D is a gain of US supplier surplus. Tariff lets US domestic firms sell more goods and increase prices.

From the US perspective, anti-dumping or countervailing duties will offset the unfair trade practice. However, on the other hand US have advantages from importing goods from China. US imports are relatively cheaper and exports are dearer. Therefore, US import deflation by importing China's goods. US consumers buy cheap China's goods and it keeps inflation in check.

From China's point of view: " Dollar hegemony prevents the exporting nations from spending domestically the dollars they earn from the US merchandise trade deficit and forces them to finance the US capital account surplus." (2) US trade deficit is funded by China's capital account inflows and it let to US economy continue to grow. US get cheap and stable source of funding its trade deficit. Therefore, US economy is growing because of China's imports in US.

Chinese currency is massively undervalued and it should revalue its fixed currency because artificially pegged currency system is beginning to hurt the Chinese. China has an "unstable" amount of reserves of American bonds and debt. However, China is able to maintain its economic growth because of export-led policy. Whether the US deficit is primarily a result of China's subsidies or is it also due to the artificially low Yuan to US $ exchange rate is debatable. Regardless, US consumers need to reduce their expenditure and the US deficit is likely to reduce. The US is an over-consuming country that needs to reduce consumption. In conclusion, although China does not follow WTO principles and US has right to haul China and put anti-dumping tariffs, the US also has advantages from the merchandise deficit with China.

24. 'Ghana AIDS Commission Launches Condom-Distribution Program Ahead Of African Cup'

This article highlights the negative affect of AIDS to the development of Human Capital in Ghana which results in worsening Economic Growth and Development.

The HIV/AIDS epidemic is a very serious problem in Ghana. From 2005 to 2006 there were "more than 300,000"[1] Ghanaians who were infected by HIV, the virus which causes AIDS. This included "21,828 children"[1]. However, HIV/AIDS problem is not only in Ghana but also in other countries mainly in Africa. See Table 1.

Table1: AFRICA and HIV/AIDS epidemic.[2]

Country	People living with HIV/AIDS	Adult (15-49) rate%	Women with HIV/AIDS	Children with HIV/AIDS	HIV/AIDS death	Orphans due to AIDS
Ghana	320.000	2.3	180.000	25.000	29.000	170.000
Mauritania	12.000	0.7	6.300	1.100	<1000	6900
Mozambique	1.800.000	16.1	960.000	140.000	140.000	510.000
Kenya	1.300.000	6.1	740.000	150.000	140.000	1.100.000
Nigeria	2.900.000	3.9	1.600.000	240.000	220.000	930.000

Table 1 shows that Ghana in comparison with Mozambique, Kenya or Nigeria is not a country which is the most harmed by HIV/AIDS epidemic. Besides, women are the most infected by AIDS. African countries contain 24.5 million people who are living with HIV while in the rest of the world there are 9.8 million people who are living with HIV [3].

AIDS increases death rate and if a country is not able to provide its population with proper nutrition, health care and medicine, the number of HIV victims will not decrease. As in Table 1 was shown a large number of people are living with AIDS.

The HIV/AIDS epidemic causes a major health and development problem in Ghana. Economic development occurs in a country when there is an increase in Real GDP per capita plus an improvement in the standard of living. It is one of the five major macroeconomic objectives. Because of AIDS Ghana is operating below PPF curve. See Figure 1.

Figure 1: Ghana is operating below its PPF.

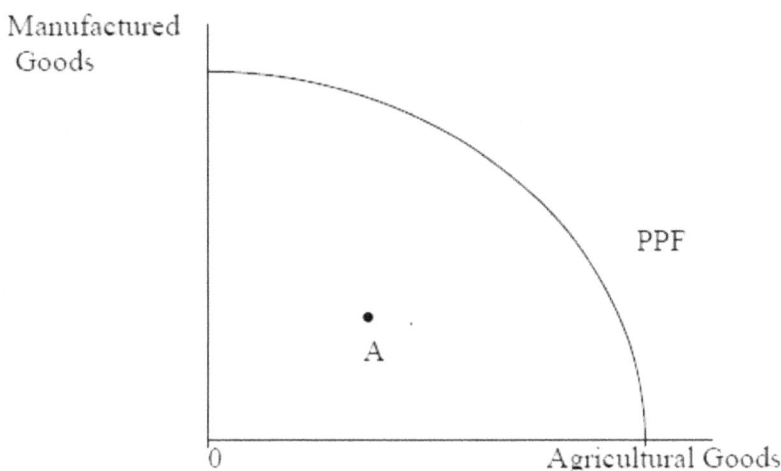

Economic growth is an increase in a country's Real GDP per capita. It is one of the five major macroeconomic objectives. A key to economic growth is quality of labour-human capital. Human capital is the investment in labour for the purpose to increase productivity, well-being and job satisfaction. The most harmful impact that has AIDS is on Human Capital.

HIV/AIDS epidemic affects economy a lot. Mainly the loss of people will affect overall economic output. AIDS epidemic affects not only the quantity of human capital but also the quality. The result of the epidemic is that HIV victims cannot work and needs significant medical care. Labour force is less productive. Children very often do not get education because they need to earn money or care for the sick family members. When children are not able to go to school the households loose future earning potential. In addition, virtually all of these people who are infected by HIV will die. Therefore, the role of health is very important for human capital in order to achieve economic stability.

The Human Development Index measures the average achievement of a country in three dimensions of human development-life expectancy at birth, adult literacy rate, and purchasing power through GDP per capita (PPP US$). According to UN 2007/2008 Human Development Report, HDI for Ghana is 0,553; life expectancy at birth is 59,1 years, education enrolment is 50,7%, adult literacy rate is 57.9% and GDP per capita 2.480$.[4]

HIV can be controlled because it is mainly transmitted through heterosexual contact. A huge number of people who are infected do not use condoms to protect themselves. Therefore, Ghana AIDS Commission is going to "distribute 5,000 condoms at no cost to hotels in Ghana accommodating African Cup guests". [5] A condom-distribution program should reduce the spread of HIV. This step is very simple, practical and is likely to be effective.

Another ways to be infected are "through blood transfusions or by using unsterilized tools".[5] In order to solve these problems Ghana needs funds for health care. Besides, the problem is that Ghana has limited resource for health. Nowadays not every Ghanaian can receive treatment when they need it. In article it is written that 21.000 people are waiting for treatment while only 11.500 are provided with it. The level of health care of a population has a major impact on the development of Human Capital.

Ghana needs investment in Human Capital. UNAIDS and WHO are working in order to reduce AIDS epidemic in countries where AIDS is distributed. UNAIDS Secretariat and WHO have analyzed that in sub-Saharan Africa there is a decline in HIV prevalence, although "the actual number of people infected with HIV continues to grow because of population growth." 6 Therefore, the progress occurs but the aim is still far.

In the conclusion, the key to Ghana's economic development is an improvement in Human capital. Short and long term solutions are required.

25. 'Bus Industry Competition Queried'

The market is controlled by few large companies as "the majority of local routes are operated by a small number of large bus companies" and the industry is an **oligopoly**, a market with a small number of large firms between which there is interdependence and each firm is affected by the decision of the rivals. Significant **barriers to entry** exist (anything that prevents or impedes the entry of firms into an industry), imperfect knowledge and the product can be differentiated, but in the bus industry is homogeneous. In some areas the market could be characterized a monopoly, "in areas where operators with a strong market position are not challenged by a large, well-resourced rival". **Monopoly** is the industry with only one large firm, possibly coexisting with much smaller ones, entry is restricted due to significant barriers to entry, unique product and imperfect knowledge. Competition in the bus industry is doubted, mainly because the "bosses" of the market are trying to increase barriers to entry, with the major barriers being aggressive tactics and possibly resource barriers. Specifically, bigger firms increase the number of routes in the areas where smaller firms are working, decreasing their demand. The form of aggressive tactics is **predatory pricing**, the pricing at a loss until competitors are forced to exit, by offering discounts for their tickets and "free rides". Possibly the oligopolistic firms agreed, informally, to limit competition by blocking new entrants, following **tacit collusion**. When competition is limited, usually inefficiency in production exists and as Fingleton suggests, "the sector was often not working as well as it should". If the oligopoly is collusive, they are considered to be functioning as a single firm, a monopoly. To show if the market is efficient, we could compare it to a more competitive market, a perfectly competitive one, as shown below.

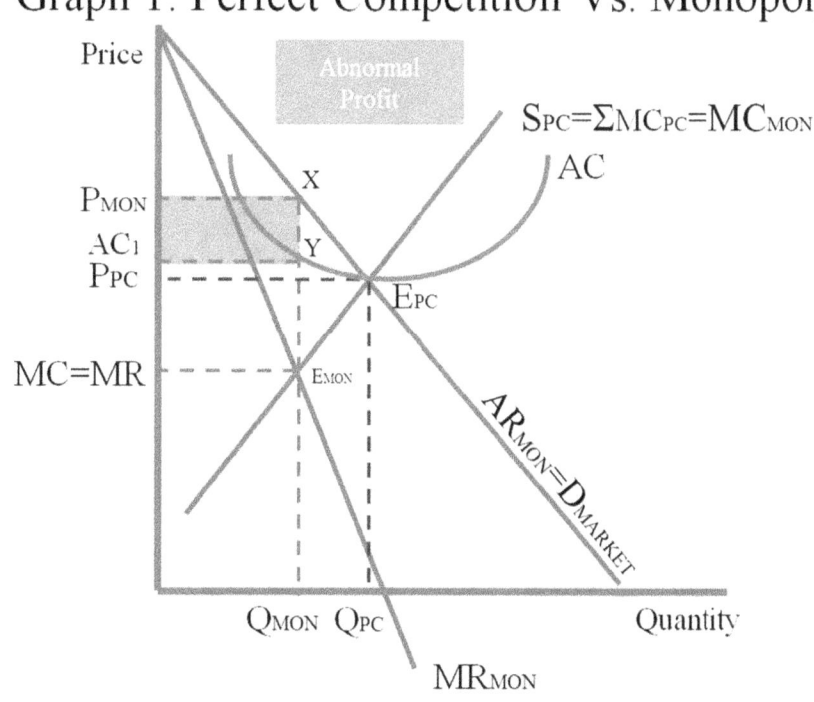

Graph 1: Perfect Competition Vs. Monopoly

If firms are profit-maximizing, they would produce were MC=MR and MC rising. Thus, the MR of the monopoly is equal to the MC of the monopoly at QMON and the price of the monopolist is PMON. Perfectly competitive firms produce QPC, because that is the output where the sum of MCs of the perfectly competitive firms, also their supply, equals the demand thus the MR. The monopolist is charging a higher price at a lower output (QPC>QMON) than the perfectly competitive firms; due to "limits on competition" higher prices are implemented, shown above as PMON>PPC. **Productive efficiency,** achieved when firms are able to produce at minimum possible average costs, as well as **allocative efficiency**, attained when producers and consumers receive maximum benefit from their resources, but neither is achieved, because as shown above, average costs for QMON are not equal to ACMIN and the price is not equal to marginal costs, PMON>MC.

The previous analysis is valid only when **economies of scale**, which exist when an increase in the scale of production, reduces all average costs of production are not evident. If there are economies of scale, Fingleton's assumption for higher prices due to limited competition is false and increasing competition in the bus industry, would make the consumer worse-off, as explained above.

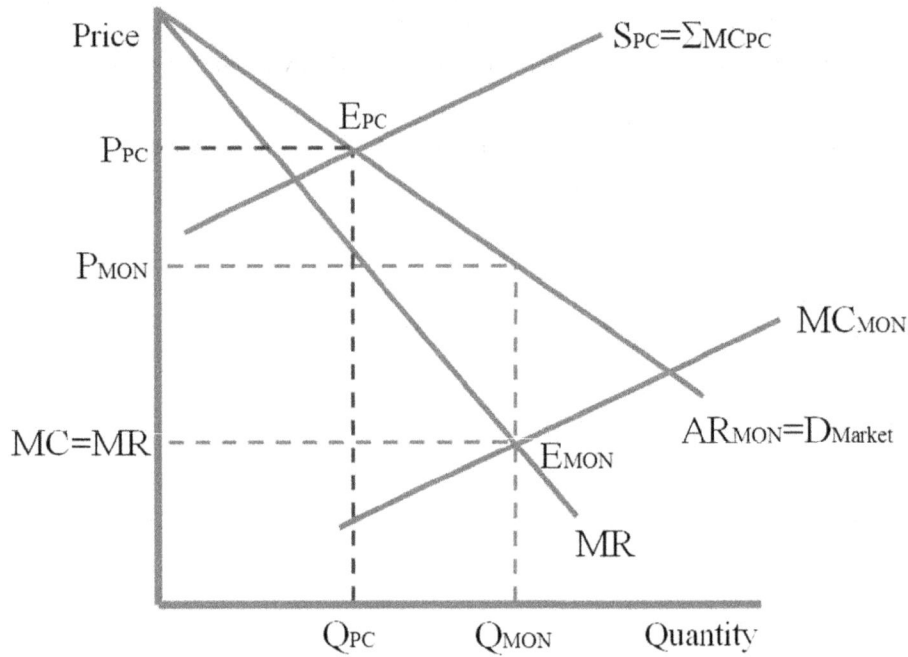

Graph 2: Perfect Competition vs. Monopoly

Because of economies of scale the monopolist would have lower marginal costs than the perfectly competitive market (MCMON<ΣMCPC). This is why the monopolist charges a price PMON lower than the perfectly competitive PPC and produced output QMON greater than QPC. Increasing competition would increase prices towards PPC against the benefit of the consumer. Also, the market may not be able to support more than the producer. In that case there is a **natural monopoly**, a situation where long-run average costs would be lower if an industry were under monopoly than if it were shared between two or more competitors.

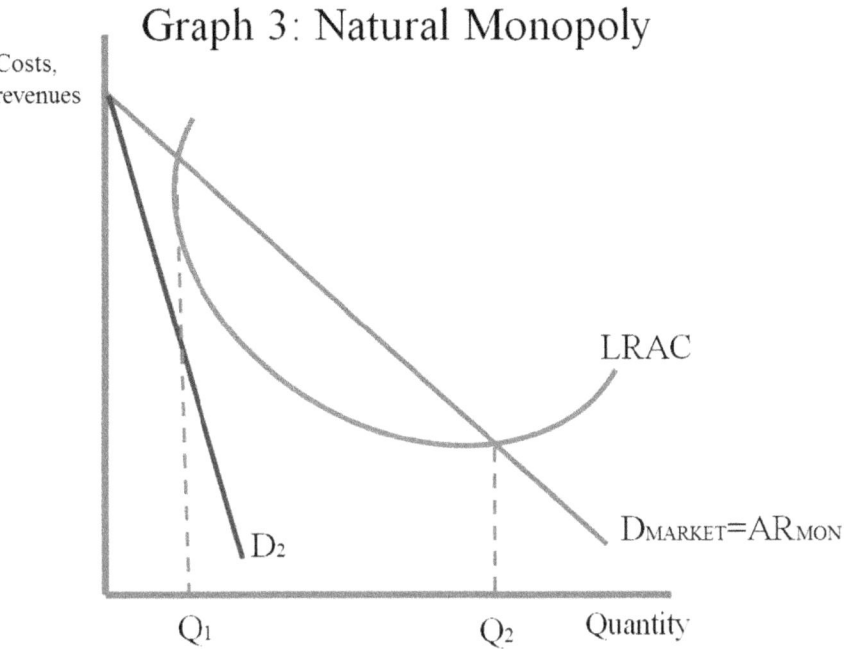

Graph 3 illustrates the industry demand curve and thus the monopolist's demand curve. One firm can serve the market profitably at an output level from Q1 to Q2. If a second firm enters, demand D2 will be faced by each of the firms when the market is evenly split, the production will be unprofitable as losses will be made at all output levels and the routes will not be served. The bus industry is subsidized with £1.2bn. Because firms are probably charging higher prices, the consumer lose by paying both the **abnormal profits**, defined as the excess of total profit above normal profit of the firms, shown at graph 1 as the area PMONXYAC1 and the subsidies through taxes.

26. 'Not By Monetary Policy Alone'

The US economy faces high unemployment rates, slow growth and falling levels of **inflation** (general and sustained increase in price levels), possibly deflation. USA is recovering, shown:

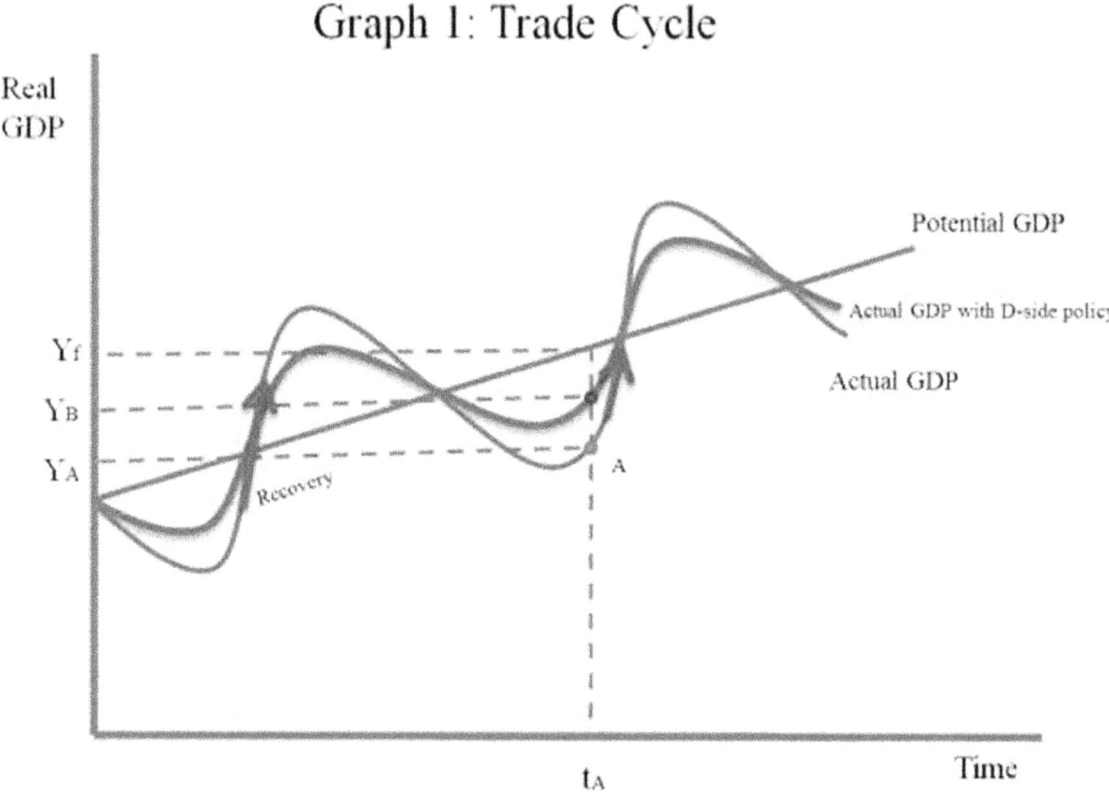

Graph 1: Trade Cycle

At tA, the economy faces a **deflationary gap**, with actual output (YA) below **full employment level of output (YF)** where all resources able and willing to work at current factor payments are employed. USA government increased **aggregate demand**(AD) (economy's total spending including consumption (C), investment (I), government spending (G) and net exports (NX)) by lowering **interest rates** (r) (price of money determining amount to be paid when borrowing or depositing), thus adopting **expansionary monetary policy** (EMP). **Quantitative easing** (QE) (central bank's money supply increase (Sm) by buying securities through open market operations) was implemented; "bringing down long-term interest rates" (graph 2). According to Classical, lower r increases **(C)** (total households' spending on goods/services over a certain time period) because falling loan payments increase money availability for consumption, durable goods consumption increases because they become cheaper and lower share prices increase financial wealth, hence consumption. According to the wealth effect theory, asset purchases -increasing asset prices - lead to increases in household wealth (consumption determinant), hence consumption. Furthermore, marginal efficiency of capital theory states that firms' **investment (I)** expenditure on capital equipment over a given time period, rises as r falls because more investment projects will be profitable and saving retained profits is less attractive.

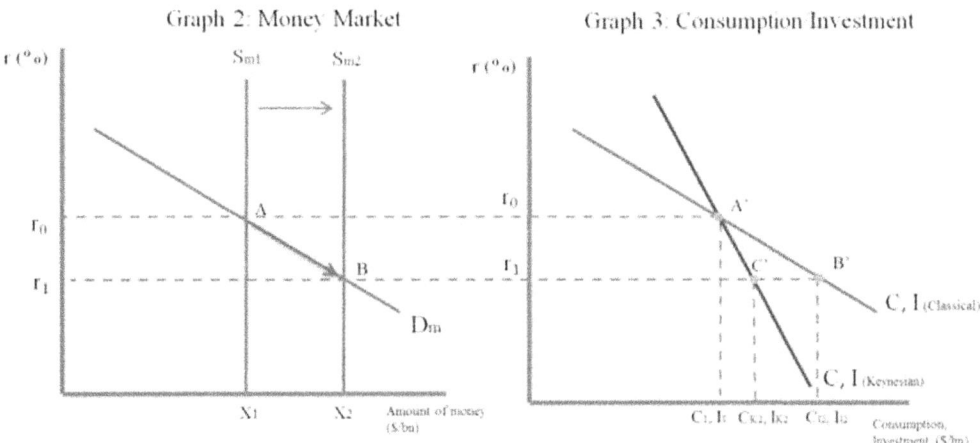

The increased (Sm) (shift of Sm1 right to Sm2) lowers r from r0 to r1, increasing C and I from C1,I1 to CI2,II2 (Classical view – C,I(Classical) curve). According to Keynes, C and I are insensitive to changes in r (inelastic C,I(Keynesian) curve) and C, I fall to C

K2,IK2<CI2,II2. Falling long-term r lower the dollar exchange rate (bring "the dollar down"), increasing (**NX**) (exports minus imports). Increasing C, I and NX leads to higher AD, reducing unemployment and preventing deflation. Falling r could "lead to a damaging rise in commodity prices" as commodities' demand increases because they are investment alternatives to long-term bonds (less attractive due to lower r).

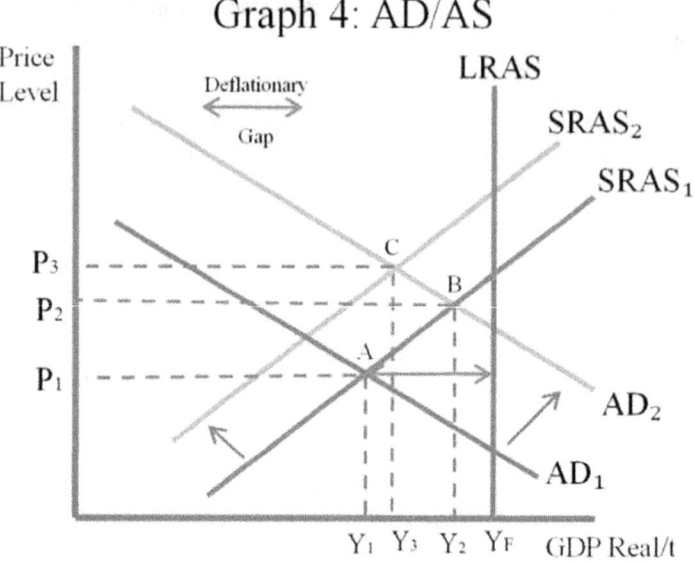

Lower r from r0 to r1, increased NX, C and I from C1,I1 to C2,I2. Their rise increases AD, from AD1 to AD2. If the economy was producing Y1 at P1, the AD rise leads to increased prices, P2, and output Y2, lowering the deflationary gap YF-Y1 to YF-Y2, reducing unemployment. But higher commodity prices increase production costs, lowering the SRAS (shift SRAS1 to SRAS2). Moving from B to C (graph 4) upsurges prices P2 to P3 and reduces output Y2 to Y3, increasing unemployment and the deflationary gap to Yf-Y3 failing to achieve the desired outcome. However, falling r lowers financial costs, thus production costs, increasing SRAS and possibly counterbalancing increased commodity prices effect, allowing SRAS stability.

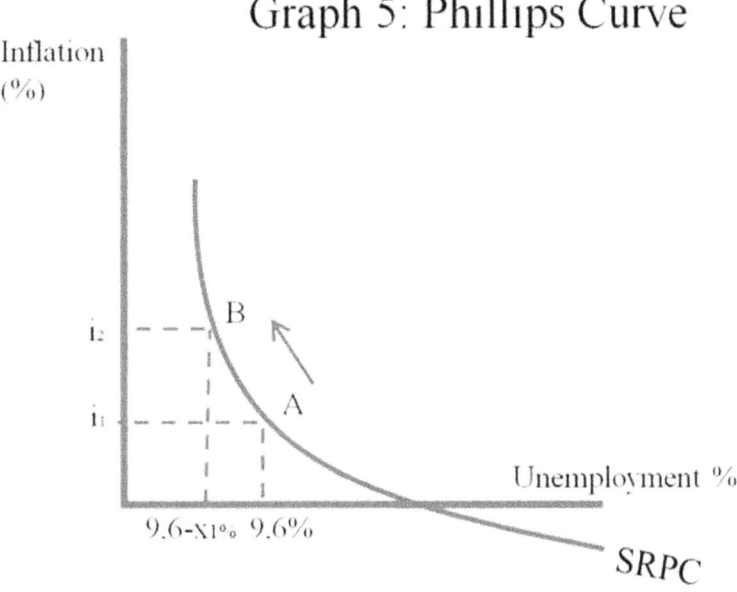

At output Y1, unemployment is 9.6% (par.2). The increase from AD1 to AD2 leads to higher prices P1 < P2 and greater output Y2, thus lower unemployment. In the Phillips curve, this is a movement from A to B, lowering unemployment to 9.6-x1% and increasing inflation rate to i2. Lower r increases output, but also lowers SRAS, reducing output and minimizing EMP's effect. Moreover, EMP increases prices P1 to P3 thus "increase fears that quantitative easing could stroke inflation" (**cost push**), by increased costs of production, and **demand pull** due to excess monetary growth, caused by increasing AD. But, with the falling inflation levels (possibly deflation), the EMP is "a potent weapon against deflation". The effect of EMP is also limited because "businesses and households are unable to borrow". Through the QE the government buys its bonds from financial institutions to encourage banks' lending. The increased Sm though, may not be used for lending but by banks to balance their sheets, making the policy ineffective. AD also increases through higher government spending and lower taxes, known as **expansionary fiscal policy (EFP)**, to "bring unemployment down faster". EFP could also strike demand-pull inflation, but initially it would not work because despite increased G and decreased taxes at a federal level, greater taxes and less spending reduced state budgets, with the one cancelling out the other. Demand side policies lead to growth (graph 1) with a movement up along the actual GDP curve, with output (Y3) being greater at tA, thus less unemployment 9.6-x1%. The EFP lowers unemployment, but expands USA's deficit. Since growth "is a serious short-term problem", it should be solved "not by monetary policy alone".

27. 'Overvalued Exchange Rate is a Sign of Britain's Economic Malaise'

During 1997-2007 the UK faced high **exchange rate (ER)**(price of one currency in terms of another) making "exports dearer, left industry struggling and there was a steady deterioration in the balance of trade". As the price of exported goods (Px) was rising faster than imported (PM), net exports (NX) fell since import expenditure increased and export revenues fell, contributing to the **current account deficit-CRAD** (total export revenues less than total import spending). Falling NX lowered aggregate demand (AD), shown by AD1 shifting left to AD2, reducing price P1 to P2 and output Y1 to Y2. Despite that, "economic growth remained robust" because lower PM, led to cheaper raw materials being imported, reducing production costs.

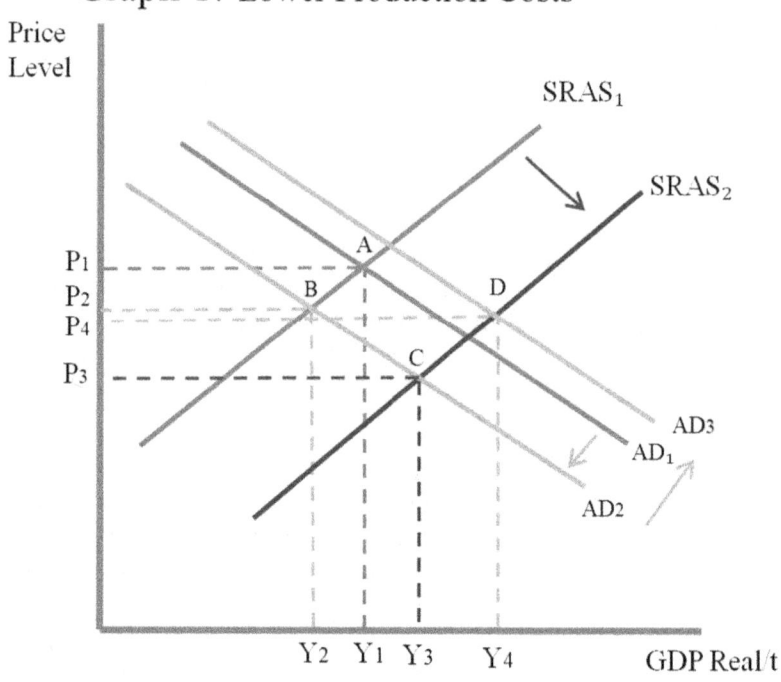

Graph 1: Lower Production Costs

Lower production costs increase SRAS, shifting SRAS1 right to SRAS2, lowering P2 to P3 and increasing Y2 to Y3 which "bore down on inflation and this helped boost consumer spending". Consumption (C) rose due to the real balance effect, as lower prices motivate consumers to lower savings to maintain real balances and since C=Yd-S, consumption rises. Also, rising SRAS lowered inflation, allowing the central bank to keep low interest rates (r), and increasing consumption (see commentary 2). The consumption increase was higher than the NX fall, therefore AD rose, shifting AD2 right to AD3, increasing P3 to P4 and Y3 to Y4. But, lower r and inflation increased consumer borrowing, thus individuals' debts, exposing them to the upcoming recession and creating unbalanced growth driven by higher C and excessive consumer borrowing.

Currently the pound's ER falls, leading to falling PX and rising PM, increasing NX. But, this assumes that depreciation will increase NX because the combined price elasticities of DX and DM are greater than one. But, if the **Marshall-Lerner condition** is not satisfied, NX will fall and export-oriented growth will not occur. Also, the government follows EMP by preserving low r and combining it with decreased ER, keeps "the cost of new investment and working capital low". Since lower r increases I and lower ER increases NX (national flow injections), based on the **multiplier**, national output could rise by a multiple of the initial injection, creating consecutive economic benefits. But, there is "upward pressure on the cost of living" due to falling purchasing power as imports become more expensive, lowering living standards. Lower r increase C and I and since NX rise, AD will increase, creating fears for demand-pull inflation. Therefore, a **contractionary fiscal policy-CFP** (lowers AD through higher *T*axes, lower *G*overnment spending) is set, lowering C due to higher T and G, allowing investment and export-oriented growth. CFP generates tax revenues used to reduce UK's budget deficit and negate fears for inflation as rising C,I,NX balances by falling C and G, allowing the Central Bank to preserve low r. With weakening pound though, more will be needed to pay back debts in foreign currencies, thus external debt rises in terms of pound. Political uncertainty, fears for delayed deficit reduction plan and low r – reducing the return on pound deposits – "make currency less attractive to global investors", averting short term capital movements, lowering pound's demand and reducing the ER.

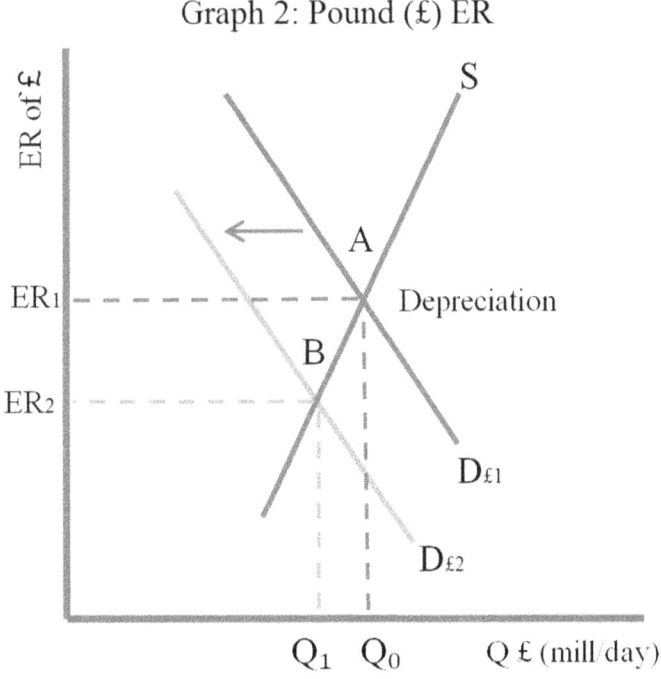

Graph 2: Pound (£) ER

Falling D£ is shown by shifting D£1 left to D£2, reducing ER1 to ER2 and Q0 to Q1 and keeping "the pound weak" to increase NX. But, since the pound's falling ER is due to fears of foreign investors by political uncertainty and suspension of deficit reduction plans, the CFP would increase investors' expectations, increasing pound's demand and the ER, obstructing economic rebalance and leading to recession. According to the **J-curve** though, depreciating reduces short term NX (worsen the CRAD) but increases NX in the long term.

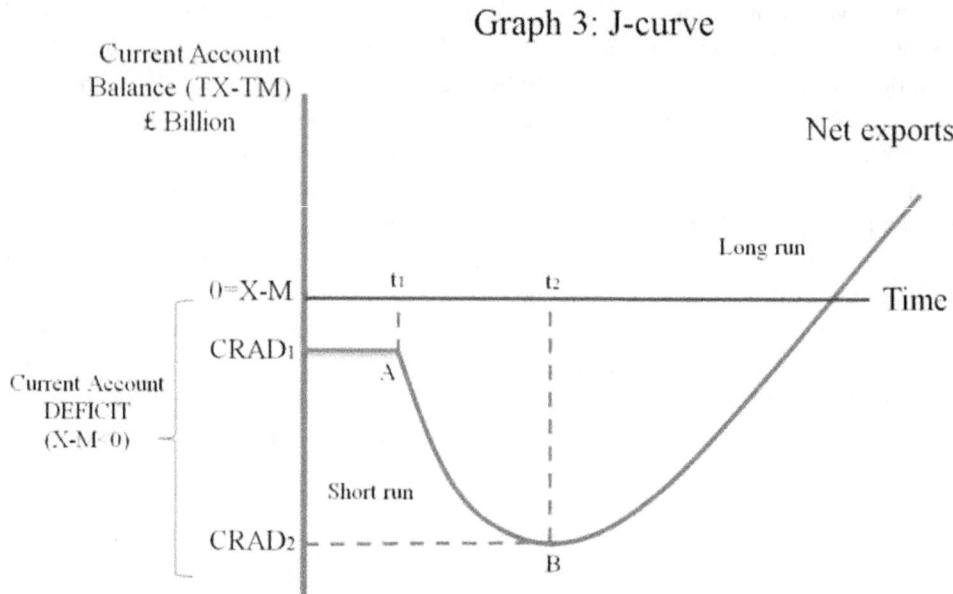

Graph 3: J-curve

Assume CRAD1 at t1 when the ER depreciates. During t1-t2 the ML-condition may not be satisfied as the price elasticities of exports and imports will probably be relatively inelastic in the short term. Therefore, falling ER reduces NX and increases CRAD1 to CRAD2, worsening foreign investors' expectations. Overall, Cameron's policy could allow UK's economy to rebalance through investment and export-oriented growth, but since falling ER 'diminished the "feel good factor", favoring the opposition parties at the election', the government might increase ER to avoid risks, even though in 2009 an overvalued pound reduced output by 5%. But, assuming that ER does fall, providing the conditions for rebalancing; this alone cannot guarantee the 'rebalance' as pound's previous devaluations had no effect due to poor quality goods, failure to control costs and lack of ambition.

www.ingramcontent.com/pod-product-compliance
Lightning Source LLC
Chambersburg PA
CBHW051213290426
44109CB00021B/2434